THE
LITTLE
BOOK
OF
IRISH
ATHLETICS

TOM HUNT

The
History
Press
Ireland

First published 2017

The History Press Ireland
50 City Quay
Dublin 2
Ireland
www.thehistorypress.ie

The History Press Ireland is a member of Publishing Ireland, the Irish Book Publishers' Association.

British Library Cataloguing in Publication Data.
A catalogue record for this book is available from the British Library.

ISBN 978 0 7509 8562 8

Typesetting and origination by The History Press
Printed by T.J. International

CONTENTS

ACKNOWLEDGEMENTS

This book documents Irish athletic excellence in mainstream events with the focus primarily on the track and field dimension of the sport. The economic, political and socio-cultural context of these achievements is also sketched.

In researching and writing this book I benefited from the expertise of many individuals especially Fiona Croke, Finbarr O'Brien, Pierce O'Callaghan, Brother John Dooley, Tommy Moloney, Jim Aughney, Robert K. Barney and Dr Patrick Bracken. Dr Bracken also provided me with access to his research on Tipperary sport in the post-Famine decades of the nineteenth century. Historians of Irish athletics are indebted to Frank Greally, Padraig Griffin and Fr Liam Kelleher for documenting the achievements of Irish athletes in their respective *Irish Runner* and *Marathon* magazine since the late 1970s. These publications were invaluable sources for this book. The works of Colm and Catherine Murphy were equally valuable.

I am indebted to the staff of the National Library of Ireland, the Local Studies section of the Central Library, Lady Lane, Waterford and the Mullingar Branch Library of the Westmeath County Library for facilitating research. Beth Amphlett's editorial input was significant; Juanita Hall accompanied the work across the finishing line and as always special thanks is due to my wife Mary for her patience and tolerance that facilitates this obsession with historical research.

1

IN THE BEGINNING

MILITARY ORIGINS

Ireland's first high-profile athletics meeting, the Curragh Encampment Garrison Races and Athletic Sports, were held on Friday, 6 June 1856 at the newly created Curragh Camp. Horse racing was staged on the previous day. A special excursion train carried patrons from King's Bridge to the Curragh on both days and patrons were offered round trips to the venue for 6s; third-class passengers paid 3s 6d for the privilege. The athletics programme, confined to officers and soldiers, consisted of two jumping events, throwing the 56lb weight, throwing the cricket ball, a 100yd flat race open to all non-commissioned officers and privates of the 2nd Brigade, a similar event for soldiers of the 3rd Brigade, a 200yd race open to all non-commissioned officers of regiments quartered at the camp, a march of 2 miles in heavy marching order, separate ½-mile races for soldiers of the 2nd and 3rd Brigades, a hopping race, a champion race of 100yd, a blindfolded bell hurdle event, a champion race of ½ mile and a hurdle race of 250yd. The meet benefited from the patronage of five officers of the British Army including General Lord Seaton, Colonel Bedford, Lieutenant Colonel Pender, Major Hillier and Colonel the Earl of Enniskillen.

These sports became a permanent feature of the recreational and social calendar of the Curragh Camp and were a major attraction for the local people of all classes. The sports organised by the 11th Hussars in 1886, for instance, attracted an attendance 'of military and friends of the regiment ... there was profuse hospitality, for which the gallant 11th was famous'; a decade later 'an immense assemblage of military and civilian on-lookers' attended what was described as the 28th annual All-Ireland Athletics meeting at the Curragh in July 1896. Musical entertainment, a reserved enclosure, the availability of food and drink, and the inclusion of novelty events were a standard feature of these days of sport and were replicated in garrison towns across the country.

Pat Bracken's work in recreating the sporting world of County Tipperary between 1840 and 1880 has established the importance of the military in the early promotion of athletic sports meetings, which were popular in the county from the 1860s. Bracken has written that 'it was no surprise to find the military leading their promotion'. In 1861, the non-commissioned officers of the 4th Hussars at Cahir Barracks organised the first recorded athletics meeting staged in the county, to commemorate the 'memorable charge at Balaklava'. The fifteen-event programme included events confined to men who fought in this famous battle. Pat Bracken's conclusion is clear-cut: 'The military were the primary instigators of early athletic sports meetings in Tipperary.'

THE COLLEGE RACES

Saturday, 28 February 1857 is another very significant date in the story of the development of modern Irish athletics. On that date, the Dublin University Football Club Races were held for the first time in Trinity College Dublin with a programme of races and novelty events such as dropping the football, throwing the cricket ball and a cigar race. The occasion attracted a huge attendance that included the lord lieutenant, the most important official in Ireland at the time. The experiment was such a success that it was repeated within a month. The College Races became an annual affair, 'the most important and fashionable gathering for athletic purposes in the world', according to one report; attendances of 20,000 were typical and in 1867 the College Races became a 2-day festival of sport, revelry and excess. The logistics of organising such an event proved difficult. The College Park at the time had no pavilion or accommodation for spectators. Marquees, seating and reserved enclosures were provided for the élite of Irish society who attended (complimentary tickets were provided for army colonels, naval commanders, judges, peers and 'county swells'). There were problems with distributing tickets, handicapping, communicating the results, keeping spectators from encroaching on the track, meeting the expectations of competitors for acceptable prizes and most of all managing the behaviour of the spectators.

The College Races were known to descend into drunkenness and riotous behaviour on occasions and the college authorities reacted by refusing permission to the athletics committee to stage the races in 1879 and 1880. This action was taken after a riot involving over 300 students took place on the second night of the 1878 races. Students had lit a bonfire using all the available wood and this included pulling down a lamp post and setting fire to the carpenter's shed. The junior dean's intervention was ignored in a tumult of horn and bugle blowing and three porters were injured in attempting to restore law and order. Those involved were punished and included in the disciplinary response was the decision to refuse permission to hold the races in 1879. Another incident occurred in April 1880 when a group of high-spirited students launched a flour bomb and firework attack on the party of the lord lieutenant as he was formally taking his leave of Ireland. As a result, permission was again withheld for the 1880 sports. The College Races resumed in 1881 as a 1-day meeting with tickets limited to 10,000 and sold to members only.

The College Races were primarily a serious athletics meet that by judicious advertising attracted some of the leading English competitors to the Dublin extravaganza. Part of the attraction was the valuable prizes on offer: the prizes for 1883 included a silver challenge cup, a claret jug, a silver salver, a Gladstone bag, opera glasses, a crocodile ink stand and an oak salad bowl. Trinity students adopted a professional approach to preparing to meet the challenge of their domestic and overseas rivals. In 1873, a trainer was recruited from the London Athletics Club and was paid 15s a day for his services. In 1881, Nathaniel Perry was recruited from the same club and was paid £12 to cover all charges and expense for his 3 weeks of work from 17 May 1881 to 7 June 1881. The association with the world of English athletics was also reflected in the adjustments made in some of the events included in the programme. The practice of using a trapeze to perform a long jump was abolished in 1872; 2 years earlier, acting on the advice of English officials, the 42lb weight was replaced by the 16lb weight as the implement of choice in weight-throwing events.

QUEEN'S COLLEGE CORK SPORTS

Athletics did not remain cloistered in places such as Trinity College Dublin and the military centres nationwide. What happened in these places was replicated in the outside world. In the 1860s and 1870s formal athletics promotions were staged in the towns and villages of Ireland. As early as February 1857 a sports day was held in Cork city that included running and jumping events, hurdle races and novel activities. The first 'Queen's Cork Athletics Sports' were staged at the Mardyke Cricket Ground on 14 May 1869; 'for the first public meeting of the kind organised under the auspices of the students, it was a great success', the *Cork Constitution* reported. The reporter was also impressed with the athletic potential on display, 'There were many possessing high ability, who with little more training, will get for them a name as well as for their cricket ability and skill and sportsmanship'. A significant feature of the fourteen-event programme was the inclusion of eight throwing and jumping events. The inclusion of the traditional Irish events represented a significant difference to the major meets staged in Dublin. The early years of the sports were dominated by many outstanding weight throwers and jumpers who were students at the college. These included John Daly, D.M. Kennedy, the great all-rounder W.A. Kelly, Terence Donovan and the legendary William 'Jumbo' Barry who entered Queen's College in 1879 to study medicine. Barry's academic career was as outrageous as his athletic talent, as during his years in the college he was never known to sit an examination and at one stage he abandoned his medical studies. He eventually enrolled in Edinburgh University where he passed all the required medical examinations over a 12-month period.

In 1870, the lord lieutenant attended; the number of running events was reduced to four and the pole vault and throwing the 16lb hammer were included in the programme. In 1871, Maurice

Davin made his debut as an athlete at a major meeting and his victory in the hammer encouraged him to focus his attention on athletics, while his brother Pat, an athletic work-in-progress, had to settle for minor placings. The English 440yd champion T.T. Hewitt (Cambridge University) was an unsuccessful competitor in 1872. Tragedy was averted in 1873 when a hammer thrower surrounded by spectators slipped and fell, but fortunately 'no one was killed or hurt. All the mischief it did was to sweep the umbrella out of a medical gentleman's hand, and finally to hit a dog in the tail', the *Cork Examiner* reported. In the mid-1870s the Queen's Cork Sports regularly attracted attendances of more than 10,000. In 1875, the entrants were so numerous that seven heats were required for both the 100yd and 440yd.

In 1863, the students of Queen's College in Galway were up and running. The Dublin Athletics Club was formed the same year. It was the most active of the Dublin clubs and promoted seven sports days in its first year, beginning on St Patrick's Day where the featured events included 'a half-mile for lads under-12', 'a one-mile race for gentlemen' and 100yd races for youths and gentlemen. The club used the College Hotel in Fleet Street as its base and concluded an agreement with the hotel's proprietor for the use of his grounds at Sackville Gardens at Summerhill Bridge for the season. These were developed and enclosed to form the City Running Grounds. Members of this club paid an annual fee of 2s 6d, which increased to 5s if not paid before a defined date; the club provided gentlemen ineligible for membership of the Dublin University Athletics Club and the later Irish Civil Service Club with an alternative opportunity to associate for athletic purposes.

The club's second programme in 1863 was staged on Easter Monday; on the same day at the Bray Cricket and Archery Grounds, a series of pedestrian and athletics events were staged under the management of John Lovett, the 'ex-champion runner of England'. After the initial foot-races-only programme, pony races were included in the Dublin Athletics Club's later promotions and, in September, the club included five weight-throwing events. These included a competition for 'putting up the 100lb dumb bell, and holding out the 56lb [weight] at arms-length for a prize of a massive gold ring'. The August meeting of 'pony racing, foot racing, weight throwing extraordinary, vaulting and other athletic feats' was open to gentlemen competitors from Ireland and Scotland.

The Dublin Catholic Young Men's Society Cricket Club staged a programme of flat races, walking matches, sack races and hurdle races. The Roundtown Sports were staged on two occasions at the Carlisle Cricket, Archery and Racing Ground at Bray; its programme of events in May included 'a half-mile race for small boys'. In June, the basic athletics programme was augmented by the staging of a flat race and hurdle race for ponies. John Lawrence promoted a series of footraces and athletic games for 'gentlemen only' open to 'all gentlemen approved by the committee'. In August, a committee of gentlemen organised 'a promenade, military band, footraces, and a grand display of fireworks' at Sandymount Cricket Ground. The Irish Civil Service Club was active from 1867, and its annual sports day for civil servants became a major addition to Dublin's social calendar. The lord mayor and lady mayoress were present in 1877 and 'at four o'clock the Lord Lieutenant, accompanied by the Duchess of Marlborough and *suite* from the Viceregal Lodge, drove into the ground ...'

The formation of the Irish Champion Athletics Club (ICAC) in 1872 by the cosmopolitan Henry Wallace Doveton Dunlop was perhaps the most significant institutional development in the 1870s. Dunlop leased a plot of land close to the Lansdowne Road Railway Station and developed a multi-purpose stadium that included a cinder running track. John Lawrence, in welcoming the development, noted that 'the absence of any ground open to all gentlemen athletes has been a great bar to training and progress in athletics'. The ICAC National Championships were staged at the venue in June 1874 and it was also used by the Dublin Amateur Athletics Club and the Irish Civil Service Club as the venue of choice for their annual sports.

The role of cricket clubs in popularising athletics was also important and many such clubs were dual-purpose cricket and athletics clubs. The Trinity College races were an outstanding financial success and the surplus was invested in providing sports facilities in the college, including a gymnasium in 1869 and the pavilion in 1884. The lesson was absorbed by other sports clubs: cricket clubs used sports days as a means of fundraising, with a charge to enter the enclosure or a makeshift grandstand, entrance fees for the events, sale of programmes and granting permission to publicans to sell liquor providing the revenue stream. Nenagh

Cricket Club, from 1875, organised an annual series of athletic sports, which were widely supported by the inhabitants of the town with 'at least two thousand spectators' regularly present.

The North of Ireland Cricket Club's annual sports, a 2-day event, was one of the leading meets in the country. Schools also organised annual meets and John Lawrence lists educational establishments such as the Armagh Royal School, where the principal was a former honorary secretary of the College Races, Portora Royal School, Portarlington School, Monaghan Diocesan School, St Mary's College Dundalk, Rathmines School and the French College as promoters of annual sports days in the 1870s for their socially élite students. The revenue generating potential was also used for philanthropic purposes. In 1863, the Sandymount Athletics Club organised at least one sports day 'for the benefit of the poor of Blackrock and Booterstown'.

The transformation of athletics from the early military, university and schools ventures into a popular participant-and-spectator sport was the sporting phenomenon of 1870s Ireland. In 1878, John Lawrence reported that 'the rapid expansion of athletics in the provinces is something remarkable ... Scarcely a village now does not go in for an athletics festival'; the *Irish Sportsman* agreed. It reported that athletics gatherings 'mushroom-like, are springing up all over the country'.

The presence of a parallel universe of popular athletics that thrived in rural Ireland provided a foundation for the formal organised meets. Athletic competition, as Paul Rouse has shown, was woven into the fabric of rural life. Across the country, where men gathered, informal contests of weight throwing, jumping and the less popular running took place. These contests took on various forms: in Cavan, men would gather weights at the end of a rope and attempt to lift them with their teeth; in Limerick, 'throwing the blacksmith's sledge' was a popular competition. As early as 1857, William Smith O'Brien entertained his tenants 'to a sumptuous repast of beef, mutton, pastries, wine, and the native, with flagons of ale', after which athletic sports and dancing were held.

Local committees were inspired by the example of the military in many places. There were no civilian-organised athletic sports meetings identified in County Tipperary prior to the military meetings. Almost immediately after the staging of the military sports in Templemore, an athletics club was formed in the town and an athletics meet was staged in August 1871 in a venue provided by the army authorities, and many soldiers competed in the events. At Fethard, military and civilian events were included on the programme and this was later replicated at Nenagh and Templemore. In the county, from 1868 to 1880, seventy-six separate athletic sports meetings were held and weight-throwing events were part of every promotion. These included civilian, military and school sports and most were organised by committees formed specifically for the purpose. Influenced by the Davin family, the town of Carrick-on-Suir emerged as a hub of athletics development in the county.

CARRICK-ON-SUIR AMATEUR ATHLETICS, CRICKET AND FOOTBALL CLUB

The surviving minute book of the Carrick-on-Suir Amateur Athletics, Cricket and Football Club (CSAACFC) provides an insight into the operation of early clubs. The club was founded on 8 August 1879 when 'an influential and highly respectable and representative body' of sixty men assembled in the County Tipperary town. The club's purpose was to promote the 'manly exercises' of football, cricket and athletics and fifty-four of the assembled became members or subscribers. In April 1880, on the proposal of Maurice Davin, amateur athletes under the age of 16 were declared eligible for membership on the payment of a yearly subscription of 5s. It is not clear if this was designed to provide additional income or promote athletics amongst the youth of the town.

This was the club of the Davin brothers and included in its membership Maurice Davin, who was appointed perpetual chairman of the executive committee. This committee included some of the town's leading professional and commercial men. A field was rented from Mrs Mary Skehan at an annual rent of £24. Some of the cost involved was recouped by renting the grazing rights of the land. A minute of 27 May 1881 recorded that Michael Quirke's offer of £1 for the grazing of the field for 4 days was accepted provided he paid a man to keep the cattle off the cricket crease and to take away what dung might be dropped near the crease! In 1883, Michael Prendergast was granted grazing rights for 'sheep only' for a sum of £7 following complaints by the cricketers that cattle damaged the crease. The club had an income of £81 6s in its first 7 months. Most of this was provided by membership fees of £37 10s (sixty-two members paid an entrance fee of 10s each and twenty-five associate members paid 5s each). Donations by various aristocrats and landed gentry provided a further £11; gate money and sale of cards for the club's athletic sports amounted to £21. Over the same period £32 was invested in rent, enclosing a playing arena and constructing a pavilion with dressing rooms and storage space.

The sale and consumption of alcohol was central to sporting occasions at the time, and the granting of space to a publican at an event was an important source of finance for meet organisers. This exercised the minds of the executive members when they organised their first sports day planned for Easter Monday 1880. An extraordinary committee meeting decided to consult the club president, W.H. Briscoe. Briscoe requested that no alcoholic drink be sold and as a result the committee decided that 'the selling or the allowing the selling of drink on that day be dispensed with'. The meet was poorly supported and following this a delegation met with Mr Briscoe to 'explain the advisability of having refreshments on the course on the day of the next meeting'. Pragmatism triumphed, Briscoe's approval was obtained and the sale of alcoholic drink, excluding whiskey and brandy, was permitted with places allocated to publicans by means of tender. The club organised three sports meets annually and at the July 1880 meet Pat Davin established a new world high-jump record when he cleared 1.90m (6' 2¾").

Sports clubs of the era tended to be short-term organisations and the Carrick-on-Suir Club conformed to the norm. An undercurrent of financial uncertainty is reflected in the minutes and financial difficulties eventually caused the winding up of the club. At a general meeting held on 16 October 1883, it was resolved to form a special committee:

> to collect all subscriptions now due and any moneys due for use of the club grounds and to sell the property of the club for the best price they can get either by public or private sale and with the money so realised to pay all the creditors in equal proportion according to the amount of their claims.

AMATEUR OR SHAM-AMATEUR?

The restriction of events to gentlemen is directly related to the amateur concept that developed in English sport in the 1860s and 1870s. John Lawrence, as an aid to clubs, published a definition of the concept in the third volume of his cricket handbook in 1868; the edition also included a copy of the laws of athletics 'never before published in Ireland'. An amateur was 'any person who has never competed in an open competition, or for public money, or for admission money' or competed with professionals for money or at any time taught or assisted in the pursuit of athletic exercises as a means of livelihood. This was an exact repetition of the definition introduced by the Amateur Athletics Club in England in 1866, which in itself was too liberal for the membership. In 1867, the definition was amended to exclude 'a mechanic, labourer, artisan or labourer' from the ranks of the amateurs and in 1868 the definition was distilled so that its first words read, 'An amateur is any gentleman ...'.

Social control, snobbery and elitism lay at the heart of the obsession with amateurism but in English athletics the barriers of class and privilege were gradually broken down and in 1880, when the Amateur Athletics Association (AAA) was established, the reference to mechanics, artisans and labourers was dropped. The restrictions on earning prize money remained but, in theory, athletics was now open to all classes.

The anti-prize money writ did not extend to Ireland and awarding money prizes for the winners of events was established practice. The Sandymount meeting of August 1863 provided the winners with the option of accepting 'prizes in money or value'. Pat Bracken's analysis of the world of Tipperary athletics in the 1870s provides a remarkable insight into the phenomenon and reveals that, between 1872 and 1878, several men earned a handsome amount of prize money by exploiting their athletic talent. At the Powerstown Sports in August 1872, William Foley of Carrick-on-Suir won three events and took home £3 in prize money for an investment of 3s in entry fees. Richard St John from Mullinahone in County Tipperary was something of a specialist in earning prize money: he competed at ten separate meetings between 1873 and 1877, and won £17 13s 6d, two cups (one valued at 30s) and a 'flask' in the thirty-two events in which he competed. In September 1875, St John made the short journey to

Carrick-on-Suir, where all the prizes on offer were monetary. The journey was worthwhile as he won three of the four events he entered and secured £5 in prize money, the equivalent of 9 weeks' wages for a farm labourer in the area. Despite his doubtful amateur status, St John competed in the ICAC National Championships in the 4-mile event in 1877. There is no reason to believe that the situation was any different in other counties.

The world of Irish athletics was not a world of clear-cut conformity. This was a concern to several of those who considered themselves to be interested parties. News had reached London by the end of the 1870s about the practice of athletes competing for money prizes. A gentleman from the London Athletics Club expressed his concern in the *Irish Sportsman*. Meetings in Ireland were 'often woefully ignorant as regards amateurs', he stated, and offered his assistance, 'If I can be of any assistance on this side of the water I shall be delighted to render any help in my power'. John Lawrence also in 1877 felt it necessary 'to warn amateurs of the danger they run of losing that title by competing with pedestrians for such [money] prizes, or with any who cannot qualify as gentleman amateurs'. In the summer of 1884, P.B. Kirwan of *Sport* and V.J. Dunbar of the *Irish Sportsman* campaigned for a greater conformity in the implementation of the rules used in promoting Irish sports meetings. This meant application of the only rules available at the time for athletic sports: those of the AAA. Both Kirwan and Dunbar were hired guns and offered their services or the services of their staff members as handicappers, judges, timekeepers or starter to organisers of sports meets. Both warned athletes of the danger of competing in athletics meetings not under AAA rules.

Rural-based athletes with ambition to compete in the more prestigious meets organised under the rules of the AAA were placed in a difficult position. Organisers of athletics meets accepted the inevitable and, by the end of the 1884 season, meetings even in small villages were organised under AAA rules. The growing trend of standardisation according to the British norm ran counter to the rising tide of Irish nationalism and the growth in support for the campaign to revive the Irish language and Irish industry.

The debate concerning eligibility to compete was largely academic, as the ability to compete in athletics and other sports was limited to those with disposable time and money. Despite the best intentions of Maurice Davin, the formation of the Gaelic Athletic Association (GAA) had little impact on the participation rates of those the founding father wished to include: 'the humble and hard-working who seem to be born into no other inheritance than an everlasting round of labour'. The practicalities of survival made such an ambition an impossible ideal.

The star athletes that emerged were members of substantial farming families or members of the professions. Tom Kiely, Percy Kirwan (AAA long jump champion1910–12) and J.J. Daly were members of families that farmed over 150 acres of good quality land. Maurice Davin combined farming with the traditional family enterprise of transporting goods on the River Suir. Pat and Tom Davin and Peter O'Connor pursued legal careers. William 'Jumbo' Barry and William Bulger were doctors; James Ryan and Walter Newburn were teachers. This was recognised by some meet promoters who included races specifically restricted to farm labourers in their programmes. In 1899, for instance, a sports organised under GAA rules included a 300yd race confined to farm labourers. Although, in theory, there was universal access to athletics, success was confined to university students and the farming, middle and professional classes.

2

MANAGING ATHLETICS (1885–1922)

IRISH CHAMPION ATHLETICS CLUB (1872–1880)

The first attempt to provide a management structure for Irish athletics was made in 1872 when the Irish Champion Athletics Club (ICAC) was established on the initiative of Henry Wallace Doveton Dunlop. Dunlop's idea was not original but was an exact replica of what had taken place in England in 1865 when the Amateur Athletics Club (AAC) was founded by John Chambers and operated as both an athletics club and a regulatory body. The AAC developed its own multi-purpose arena at Lillie Bridge in London, which opened in 1869 with facilities for athletics, cricket, cycling, football, tennis, as well as possessing its own stables and hotel for visiting sportsmen.

The primary purpose of the ICAC, open to all 'gentlemen Irish amateurs', was to organise an annual end-of-season national championship for athletics; it also functioned as a club for athletes. The rejection of a plan to develop a running track in the grounds of Trinity College Dublin inspired the entrepreneurial Dunlop to look elsewhere, and in December 1872 he leased a plot of land close to the Lansdowne Road Railway Station from the Earl of Pembroke.At the end of its first season, John Lawrence, in his *Handbook of Cricket in Ireland*, reported on the progress of the development work on creating a multi-purpose sports venue: 'enclosed ground, first running path in Ireland laid, cricket ground, hurdle course, archery ground, four hundred seat grandstand erected, sloping seats for six hundred more, archery and croquet hut, Gate lodge, Dressing room under the railway arch'. It was a remarkable development and enabled Dublin to participate fully in the modern world of sport. On 5 June 1876, the Lansdowne Road venue hosted the first athletics international in the history of the sport, between Ireland and England, and on 11 March 1878 the ground hosted the first of many rugby internationals.

The ICAC acted as an umbrella body for existing clubs and the Civil Service Club, Trinity College Dublin, the Queen's Colleges and schools such as the Royal Portora College in Enniskillen affiliated. Eighteen high-profile patrons representing 'every phase of politics, creed and social position', according to a contemporary report, including the Lord Chancellor of Ireland, five earls, two lords and several high-order military officers supported the new club. Its committee also included representatives from Armagh, Belfast, Cork, Galway, Limerick and Lurgan. The first Irish championships organised by the ICAC were held on Monday, 7 July 1873 at College Park in Trinity College Dublin. The winners of the thirteen championships staged were awarded perpetual trophies with a design based on classical themes. Silver and bronze medals were also awarded to the winners and second-placed athletes. The event attracted an attendance of 'about 8,000' spectators and ninety-one 'gentleman amateurs' competed. Matthew Stritch was the outstanding athlete and won three titles in the weight-throwing events, with Maurice Davin the runner-up on each occasion. There was consolation for the Davin family, however, as Tom Davin won the high-jump title with a leap of 1.785m (5' 10¼"), a world best at the time.

The 1874 championships were staged at Lansdowne Road, which remained the venue for the championships during the lifetime of the ICAC. After staging the 1880 championships, the ICAC was dissolved and its property and trophies were used to discharge its liabilities. Poorly attended and supported national championships were staged in 1881, organised by an ad-hoc committee of interested parties and by the Dublin Amateur Athletics Club (1881–1884).

GAELIC ATHLETICS ASSOCIATION (1884)

Michael Cusack was a central figure in the Dublin athletics community as an official, commentator and competitor. His achievements included winning the national shot-put title in 1881. A native of County Clare, Cusack qualified as a teacher in 1866 and he founded the Cusack Academy in Dublin in 1877, an establishment that specialised in preparing students for the examinations that provided the entry route to the service of the British Empire. The recreational needs of the students were catered for by the establishment of the short-lived Cusack Academy Football Club, which was affiliated to the Irish Rugby Football Union. Cusack described himself as 'a sterling lover of the game' and multi-tasked as club secretary, trainer and teak-tough forward. In the 1881–1882 season, his last in the game, he lined out for the Phoenix Rugby Club. He was also a lover of cricket and in 1882 wrote that the sport was Ireland's national game and that every town and village in Ireland should have its own cricket club. However, soon after he retired from rugby, he also abandoned cricket, became a founder member of the Dublin Hurling Club and turned his attention to the revival of hurling and the reform of Irish athletics.

The demise of the ICAC coincided with a time when athletics in Britain was placed on a sounder footing with the establishment of the Amateur Athletics Association (AAA) at the Randolph Hotel, Oxford on 25 April 1880. In the void created by the collapse of the ICAC and the failure of a robust alternative to emerge, the AAA became the effective regulatory body for Irish athletics, and it became the norm that athletics meetings in Ireland should be organised under AAA rules. These rules were promoted by the two main sports newspapers of the day. P.B. Kirwan of *Sport* made members of his staff available to officiate at any athletics meeting in the country and had the rules of the AAA published in his paper. V.J. Dunbar of the *Irish Sportsman* also offered his services and travelled widely to officiate at athletics meets promoted under AAA rules. Michael Cusack reacted to this with fanatical zeal. AAA rules tended to favour running rather than the throwing events, which Cusack believed were more appropriate to the Irish character. The rules of the AAA carried a strong class bias and their concept of amateurism excluded those who had competed for cash prizes, as we have seen. The trend of staging athletics meets on a Saturday and during midweek became the norm and placed severe limitations on those who could compete.

Cusack's carefully orchestrated propaganda campaign on the need to reform and democratise Irish athletics reached its climax on 11 October 1884 when his seminal article 'A Word about Irish Athletics' was published in two weekly nationalist journals, *United Ireland* and *Irishman*, a contribution considered by his biographer Marcus de Búrca to be 'beyond doubt the most effective single piece of writing Cusack ever did'. Cusack called on 'Irish people to take the management of their games into their own hands, to encourage and promote in every way every form of athletics which is peculiarly Irish, and to remove with one sweep everything foreign and iniquitous in the present system'. Cusack argued that it was time to end the situation whereby athletics meetings were held 'under the rules of the Amateur Athletics Association of England, and that any person competing at any meeting not held under these rules should be ineligible to compete elsewhere'. He also claimed that every effort was made to make the meetings look as English as possible with 'foot races, betting, all flagrant cheating being their most prominent features. Swarms of pot-hunting mashers sprang into existence.'

In a clearly choreographed reaction, a week later, Maurice Davin responded and offered his support and modestly agreed to 'gladly lend a hand if I can be of any use'. He was less hysterical than Cusack and more measured in his response, 'The code of the AAA was a good one and in the management of Irish athletics and games they could not do better than adopt rules similar; and if they sent men over to England to compete he knew they would be well received there …'. Davin was concerned at the absence of jumping and weight-throwing events at 'what might be called leading meetings', as it was his experience that 'for one bystander who takes off his coat to run a foot race, forty strip to throw weights or try a jump of some kind'. Davin expanded on Cusack's brief to include the revival of hurling and Gaelic football 'under regular rules' as 'there are no rules, and, therefore, these games are often dangerous'.

Davin was one of the most respected figures in Irish athletics at the time. He was the holder of ten Irish championship titles in weight-throwing events earned between 1875 and 1879 under the auspices of the IAAC and he stepped out of retirement in 1881 and won AAA titles in hammer throwing and the shot-put. A successful farmer and businessman who operated a river transport company on the River Suir, he competed successfully at rowing before turning his attention to athletics. He prepared meticulously for the sport and developed his own weight-lifting programme to enhance his natural strength, he was careful with his diet and was a non-drinker who abhorred smoking.

On 27 October 1884 a letter signed by Cusack and Davin was published in the *Freeman's Journal* and *The Irish Sportsman* inviting interested parties to a meeting in Thurles 'to take steps for the formation of a Gaelic Association for the preservation and cultivation of our National Pastimes and for providing rational amusement for the Irish people during their leisure hours'. The meeting was held on 1 November 1884, and at Lizzie Hayes' Commercial Hotel in Thurles, the Gaelic Athletics Association for the Preservation and Cultivation of National Pastimes (GAA) was established.

It was generally accepted that seven men attended the meeting but in recent times a compelling argument has been made for the presence of thirteen men. These have been identified as Michael Cusack, Maurice Davin, John Wyse Power, J.K. Bracken, John McKay, Joseph Ryan, St George MacCarthy, William Foley, T.K. Dwyer, Charles Culhane, William Delahunty, Michael Cantwell and John Butler. All shared a history of involvement in sport, either as competitors or administrators.

Davin addressed the meeting and spoke of the need to establish an organisation that would organise Irish sport for Irish people using Irish rules. He was elected first president of the association; Cusack, Wyse Power and McKay were appointed secretaries and Archbishop Croke, Michael Davitt and Charles Stewart Parnell were invited to become patrons of the new association. In the months that followed, Maurice Davin framed the rules for hurling and effectively invented the game of Gaelic football, but the new association concentrated on athletics for the first 18 months or so of its existence. Rules were prepared to cater for throwing and jumping events; the accepted AAA practices were adopted for running events. Crucially there were no prohibitions on Sunday play and this theoretically brought organised sport within the reach of those previously excluded from the arena. In January 1885, to strengthen its control of athletics, a rule was passed that declared athletes who competed at meetings organised under laws other than those of the GAA ineligible to compete at meetings held under its auspices. The formation of the GAA alarmed those who had been associated with the promotion of what might be termed the élite athletics events in Dublin, and after several years without a controlling body Irish athletics was soon to have two rival bodies engaged in a struggle for the management of the sport.

IRISH AMATEUR ATHLETICS
ASSOCIATION (1885–1922)

The Irish Amateur Athletics Association (IAAA) was established at a meeting held in the Wicklow Hotel, Dublin on Saturday, 21 February 1885. Thirty-four representatives of athletics clubs and associations attended, including Michael Cusack as the representative of Maurice Davin. Letters of support were received from clubs that were unable to send delegates to the meeting. John Dunbar was elected honorary secretary of the new association; its objectives were to govern and encourage amateur athletics in Ireland, to improve the management of athletics and provide uniformity of rules for the guidance of local committees, to deal repressively with any abuses and to hold annual championships. The IAAA's competitions were confined to amateur athletes and its rules included the following definition of an amateur:

> An amateur is one who has never competed for a money prize or staked a bet or run with or against a professional for any prize or who has never taught, pursued or assisted in the practice of athletic exercises as a means of obtaining a livelihood.

This was an exact replica of the AAA's definition and was also the rule adopted by the GAA in 1885 in its first set of rules for athletics. However, the GAA included a pragmatic response to the realities of the day by allowing amateur athletes to compete for money prizes of limited value, to offset their travelling expenses. It was hard to argue against the logic of this rational compromise, as explained by Michael Cusack: instead of giving prizes such as fish knives and butter coolers it was far more sensible for 'a poor Irish youth to accept his travelling expenses and a sovereign or two to get the fish or butter'. The officials of the IAAA also included a stipulation that any athlete competing in a non-IAAA-approved competition 'shall be disqualified from competing at any sports held under IAAA Laws'.

A struggle for the control of Irish athletics began immediately and continued with increasing intensity throughout 1885. In the words of Paul Rouse, 'The row was an extraordinary blessing for the GAA' as it provided the association with 'a level of publicity and status it could scarcely have dreamed of following the damp squib of its inaugural meeting'. The GAA depicted itself as nationalist and democratic and at the same time stigmatised the IAAA as pro-British and elitist. Michael Cusack availed of the opportunity to indulge in his capacity to insult and antagonise. The IAAA was a 'ranting, impotent, West British abortion', he wrote. John Dunbar's attempt at conciliation was dismissed abruptly: 'Dear Sir, I received your letter this morning and burned it'.

The IAAA was the first to organise its national championships and a sixteen-event championship was staged at the RDS Showgrounds in Ballsbridge, Dublin on 11 July 1885; the GAA's equivalent did not take place until 6 October at the racecourse in Tramore, County Waterford. By this time, the GAA had emerged as the dominant force in Irish athletics and at its annual meeting, held in late October, Michael Cusack reported that close to 150 meetings were held under GAA rules. The formation of the GAA transferred the control of athletics in the provinces to local nationalists, many of them active politically, and at the same time hurling and Gaelic football matches were organised on a countrywide basis.

The first serious trial of strength between the two rival athletics bodies took place in Tralee, County Kerry. The County Kerry Amateur Athletics and Cricket Club (CKAACC) staged its annual sports on 17 June 1885, on the same day as the town branch of the GAA organised its sports. Michael Cusack lent his organisational expertise to the GAA club and spent time in Tralee supporting the local committee and securing nationalist and clerical support for the show trial. The GAA event was an extraordinary success: 'the entries amounted to the unprecedently large numbers of four hundred and sixty-four ... the people came swarming in from every part of the country,' *United Ireland* reported. Over 10,000 spectators reportedly attended, with only a few hundred present at the CKAACC promotion 'although the large stand was well filled with the elite of the county'.

The first of many splits in Irish athletics ended in April 1886 when the GAA removed its rule permitting money prizes at athletics meets and the IAAA reciprocated by declaring that all athletes were eligible to compete in its competitions unless they had competed for money prizes. It also agreed to recognise GAA suspensions and stipulated that all athletes had to be members of either the GAA or the IAAA to compete in its events. The agreement, at times uneasy, survived for 20 years, and because of the rapprochement Irish athletes had the opportunity of competing in a wide programme of events and in two national championships. The high point of this spirit of cooperation was the Joint Committee of the associations, which adjudicated on performances and ratified new national records.

The distinctions between the two organisations were more complex than the mere political: while the GAA's membership embraced the full spectrum of nationalist opinion, the IAAA was more politically inclusive and some of its leading members were firm believers in the unity of Great Britain and Ireland as a single political entity. The GAA predominated in rural Ireland, whereas the IAAA was principally an urban institution with a Dublin power base and a significant presence in Belfast. The GAA prioritised the traditional pastimes of rural Ireland, jumping and weight throwing, while the IAAA favoured the running events. Sunday track-and-field meets were strictly prohibited by the IAAA, a constraint that inevitably limited its influence in rural Ireland and its class appeal, although its member athletes were free to compete on Sundays in GAA events.

Both organisations rejected the opportunity to compete at the Athens Olympic Games of 1896. Daniel Bulger and James Magee represented the IAAA at the Sorbonne Conference in 1894, at which the modern Olympic Games were revived, but there is no evidence available of their contribution, if any, to the conference. The IAAA certainly received an invitation, but there is no evidence that the GAA was directly invited. There was hardly a GAA to invite. The games were staged at a time when the organisation was at its weakest and in need of life support. In the mid-1890s, it appeared to be in an advanced stage of terminal decline as the fallout from the Parnell split, emigration and economic depression pushed it to the brink of extinction.

The IAAA, in association with its Scottish equivalent, organised a 1-day international match that continued in an unbroken sequence until 1913; in 1914, a triangular contest was made possible when England joined. The first was staged at the Celtic Football Club's Park Head grounds, Glasgow on 20 July 1895 and initiated what was the world's first regular series of international matches; Ireland triumphed in the initial encounter (6–5) and had a more convincing victory in the second international (7–4) at Ballsbridge, witnessed by an attendance of 3,000.

Selection of the Ireland team was based on performance in the IAAA National Championships, which on occasion upset some athletes, most notably the great long jumper, Peter O'Connor, who was not selected in 1902, much to his chagrin. The IAAA's National Championships continued until 1914, when they were postponed for the duration of the First World War. The championships resumed in 1919 and were last held in 1922. The GAA Championships continued without interruption from 1885 until 1922 but from the early 1900s Gaelic football and hurling dominated the association's business.

Neither the GAA nor the IAAA was affiliated to the International Amateur Athletics Federation (IAAF). The United Kingdom of Great Britain and Ireland was admitted to membership of the IAAF at its inaugural meeting, held in Berlin in August 1913, with the AAA the recognised national athletics federation. The IAAA was essentially a subcommittee of the AAA with responsibility for managing athletics on the island of Ireland.

3

MANAGING THE SPORT (1922–2017)

A NEW POLITICAL REALITY

The temporary postponement of the IAAA's National Championships for the expected short-term duration of the First World War stretched into 4 years. At the outbreak of the war, what was to become Ireland's decade of revolution was already underway and ended in 1923 with the conclusion of the catastrophic Civil War. The tumultuous decade finished with the island of Ireland divided into two separate political entities: the twenty-six-county Irish Free State, a self-governing dominion of the British Empire with the same constitutional status as Canada, and the six-county, semi-autonomous Northern Ireland within the United Kingdom. The nationalist community was now bitterly divided between those for whom the concept of a single-state Ireland was a non-negotiable concept and those who were prepared to adopt a more pragmatic approach to achieving Irish unity. The island of Ireland also contained a significant unionist community for whom Irish independence from Britain was an alien concept.

The new political landscape's impact on athletics was greater than on any other sport. Most national federations managed to maintain unity by considerable compromise as issues of political symbolism were tailored to accommodate diverse political and cultural interests. Athletics administrators were unable to make this leap of faith and the promotion of the sport suffered irreparable damage as a result.

NATIONAL ATHLETIC AND CYCLING ASSOCIATION OF IRELAND (NACAI)

J.J. Keane was the architect of a fragile athletics unity achieved by the establishment of the NACAI as the single controlling body of athletics and cycling on the island in 1922. Keane persuaded the GAA to abandon its nominal interest in athletics and worked closely with Dr Robert Rowlette (president of the IAAA, 1908–1920), who played the lead role in persuading the IAAA to also disband. In May 1922, a special GAA Congress recommended the adoption of Keane's scheme and the National Athletics and Cycling Association of Ireland (NACAI) was established. Quietly and without fuss the GAA had euthanised its involvement in athletics. At a special congress of the IAAA in July 1922 a proposal that the IAAA cease to exist was adopted. The formation of the NACAI was approved, as was a resolution recommending that clubs affiliated to the IAAA join the new association.

Unity was not immediate. J.J. Keane was a strong supporter of the GAA's exclusion rules and these rules were echoed in the new athletics body. British soldiers, navy men and police on active service in Ireland were declared ineligible for membership of the NACAI. This was unacceptable to some Belfast clubs, who formed the Amateur Athletics Association of Ireland to cater for those that refused to join the NACAI. J.J. Keane was again responsible for the final initiative that made unity possible and successfully proposed the removal of the rule barring foreign soldiers, sailors or police from competing in NACAI competitions. A period of intense negotiations between the several interested parties in Northern Ireland with the NACAI followed. The NACAI went about its business and the first international triangular contest between Ireland, England and Scotland under its auspices was held in Stoke-on-Trent on 16 July 1923.

The negotiations were successfully concluded and the agreements were ratified at the first congress of the NACAI held on 11 May 1924 at the Clarence Hotel (Dublin), although no Ulster delegates attended. All amateur athletes resident in Ireland were now eligible to join the NACAI irrespective of political or devotional allegiance. International selection would be based on form shown in the national championships and, as far as possible, in the new spirit of inclusiveness, these championships would be held on Saturdays and Sundays on alternative years. Delegates attending the conference received more good news from Keane, who confirmed that international recognition had been granted by the IAAF. The NACAI application for membership was approved by the IAAF Executive Council in January 1924 and at the seventh congress of the IAAF held in Paris on 4 July 1924, Ireland was elected to membership of the IAAF along with Greece, Argentina, Japan and Uruguay. For the first time since 1885, the control of athletics (including cross-country running) and cycling in Ireland was vested in a single body. Unfortunately, the arrangement quickly unravelled.

THE NORTHERN IRELAND AMATEUR ATHLETICS ASSOCIATION (NIAAA)

Ireland as a thirty-two-county entity was a fully involved member of the IAAF during the 1920s and the AAA had no difficulty with this position. Membership of the IAAF also brought responsibilities, and when the NACAI officers implemented IAAF policies a series of events began that ended with the suspension of the association from the IAAF. The rules prohibiting gambling, dog and pony races and granting membership to professional clubs were implemented and this was especially significant for Belfast clubs, especially the Belfast Celtic Football Club. These clubs withdrew from the NACAI and founded the Northern Ireland Amateur Athletics, Cycling and Cross-Country Association (NIAACCCA) in July 1925. What was a domestic dispute soon took on an international dimension and became politicised. Unionist-minded administrators and Northern Ireland politicians used the opportunity presented by the dispute to pursue their agenda to achieve separate recognition for Northern Ireland in sport.

Attempts to broker an agreement failed and on 30 December 1929 several clubs unanimously decided to form a Northern Ireland branch of the AAA. The NIAAA became the latest organisation with a managerial and promotional role in Irish athletics when the AAA approved the decision in April 1930. The affiliation of Great Britain to the IAAF was now defined to mean the affiliation of the United Kingdom of Great Britain and Northern Ireland, a situation that has remained unchanged to this day. The AAA delegated to the new northern body 'full powers to control amateur athletics in the area known as Northern Ireland' and attempted to limit the NACAI's jurisdiction to the 'area known as the Irish Free State'.

This was totally unacceptable to the officials of the NACAI, who protested to the IAAF at what was regarded as AAA interference. The first response of the IAAF's president Sigfrid Edström suggested that the NACAI's claim to all-island jurisdiction was unlikely to continue. 'Formerly your association governed all Ireland, but since the formation of the Irish Free State things have been different and we must live up to modern time,' he informed J.J. Keane. The powerful Edström believed that political boundaries and the boundaries of national athletics federations should coincide.

A special council meeting held in London in May 1931 between the Executive Council of the IAAF and officials of the NACAI and the AAA failed to resolve the difficulty; negotiations held in Belfast early in 1932 between the NIAAA and NACAI officials did produce an agreement that recommended the establishment of autonomous bodies in the Irish Free State and Northern Ireland, which would unite to form a single twelve-member body to manage national and international events. A neutral flag depicting the arms of the four provinces 'on a field of St Patrick's Blue' was to be flown at international events. NACAI delegates accepted this agreement at a special congress with a key amendment that the tricolour would be the flag used for all international events. This was unacceptable to the NIAAA and more Belfast clubs severed their connection with the NACAI after the decision.

The post-Olympic IAAF Congress in Los Angeles chose not to discuss the matter but the international federation's congress held in Stockholm on 28–29 August 1934 amended its constitution and resolved the matter to the satisfaction of the IAAF and the AAA. A definition of a country as 'a land under a particular sovereignty or government' was approved and the jurisdiction of members of the IAAF was limited to the political boundaries of the country or nation they represented. The British Amateur Athletics Board, as the body responsible for managing athletics in Great Britain and Northern Ireland, was also approved for membership of the IAAF. This decision meant that, according to the rules of the IAAF, the NIAAA was now responsible for managing athletics in Northern Ireland and the jurisdiction of the NACAI was limited to the territory of the Irish Free State.

THE NACAI OPTS FOR ATHLETICS ISOLATION

The choice presented to officials of the NACAI was simple but laced with political implications. If they wished to continue as the internationally recognised body for the management of Irish athletics, they would have to confine their activities to the Irish Free State. A special congress to discuss the matter was held on 6 October 1934 and voted 31–23 to reject the IAAF decision, a decision that was later confirmed in February 1935 at the annual congress (27–24). J.J. Keane, in his final significant contribution to Irish athletics, spelled out the implications of such a decision prior to the annual congress. In a powerful analysis, he pointed out that it 'was the best interests of the rest of the country to devote all our attention to the welfare of athletics within the political boundaries'. A failure to accept the IAAF's constitutional amendment would mean that 'the North will carry on with a free hand, the British Association will continue to recognise them' and the IAAF 'will not suffer in any way through the absence of an Irish delegation'. Athletics isolation was inevitable and athletes such as the 1932 Olympic champions Bob Tisdall and Pat O'Callaghan 'will no longer be able to make the name of Ireland ring in the ears of the world'. The Tailteann Games would end as 'no athletes can come here from any other country'. Keane appealed to the congress delegates not to let 'political considerations' influence their decision: 'It is not a question of politics, it is a question of the future of Irish athletics.'

Unfortunately for the future development of the sport, delegates for the second time opted to prioritise the political dimension. The idea that the Irish formed a single nation was a fundamental tenet of Irish nationalism. In the context of the time, a vote to accept the new IAAF reality meant recognising the border and the division of the island. This was impossible for principled nationalists such as Dr Eamonn O'Sullivan, who argued that the loss of international competition, which involved only a small number of athletes, was a small price to pay for national unity.

The implications of the NACAI decision quickly became apparent and it was suspended from membership of the IAAF effective from 1 April 1935. Officials were informed that its members were ineligible to take part in any international competition or to receive foreign athletes to compete in the Irish Free State.

AMATEUR ATHLETICS UNION
OF ÉIRE (AAUE) 1937–1967

Isolation from the international arena, and especially the absence from the 1936 Berlin Olympic Games, focused the pragmatic minds of some Dublin-based NACAI officials. In November 1936, Bo Ekelund, secretary of the IAAF, revealed that a new Irish association had enquired about the possibility of affiliation to the IAAF and had indicated its willingness to accept its rules. Opportunities were given to the NACAI to comply with the IAAF regulations but when the final deadline of 15 May 1937 expired, the NACAI 'was suspended forever and expelled from membership of the IAAF'.

Clonliffe Harriers severed its connection with the NACAI in March 1937 and Fearons' AC was next to jump from the isolationist ship. They were joined on 10 April by Donore Harriers. O'Callaghan's Mills AC (Clare) became the first rural club to break with the NACAI and three more Dublin clubs, City and Suburban Harriers, Dublin University and the Hospitals' Trust Club severed their connections in mid-April. A new athletics body, the Irish Amateur Athletics Union, prepared to accept the IAAF, rules was established on 22 April 1937, at a meeting held at Moran's Hotel, Dublin. Representatives of three of Dublin's leading clubs, Donore Harriers, Clonliffe Harriers and City and Suburban Harriers attended. The new association was granted provisional membership of the IAAF in May 1937 pending the holding of the IAAF Congress in Paris on 28 February 1938, where it was granted full membership. The new association's representatives pointed out that since the application for membership was submitted a new Irish Constitution had been adopted, and to reflect this change the new affiliate was to be known as the Amateur Athletics Union of Éire (AAUE). This was accepted and the AAUE was elected to the IAAF as the representatives of the twenty-six-county Ireland.

The AAUE immediately initiated a programme of events: the first interclub contest took place on 29 May, twelve AAUE athletes travelled to Belfast to compete in the RUC Sports in June; the AAUE and the NIAAA contested a match in August and the first AAUE National Championships were held at Lansdowne Road on 30 August 1938. It was business as usual for the NACAI as its domestic programme continued in splendid international isolation. Athletics on the island was now controlled by three federations that broadly reflected the political divisions of the island: the uncompromising nationalist NACAI, the unionist-minded NIAAA and the more pragmatic, moderate nationalist and IAAF-recognised AAUE. This situation remained unchanged until 1967 despite attempts made to achieve unity.

UNITY TALKS

Various attempts were made to negotiate a settlement over the next 30 years. The first, in 1946, involved the three associations and promised much but was eventually foiled by the intransigence of the IAAF honorary secretary, E.J. Holt, who was unable to circumvent 'the limitations as regards the "nation" clause in the I.A.A.F. rules'. The late 1940s and 1950s were a period of extreme bitterness between the AAUE and the NACAI and the decision of the County Tipperary club Coolcroo to join the AAUE added to the tensions. Irish Olympic Council meetings provided a forum for both associations to articulate their animosities with the result that both were excluded from membership in 1952.

The AAUE attracted little popular support and its influence was confined to the Dublin region. In 1956, the AAUE had a membership of approximately 300 athletes attached to eight clubs; the NACAI's 380 clubs included a membership of close to 4,500. The affiliation of the AAUE to the IAAF restored international athletics competition to the Republic of Ireland and enabled its members to compete in international events. In 1946, over 8,000 spectators were present in College Park to see the great English athlete Sidney Wooderson in action; in 1949, the International Cross-Country Championships were staged at Baldoyle Racecourse in Dublin where the great French runner Alain Mimoun dominated the field.

Lord Killanin became president of the Irish Olympic Council in 1951 with an ambition to achieve athletics unity. He also replaced J.J. Keane as the member of the International Olympic Committee. In 1954 Lord Killanin, with Major General W.R.E. Murphy and Chief Superintendent Patrick Carroll, held discussions with Thomas Cullen (president of the NACAI) and Freddie Moran (president of the AAUE), and later with officials of the NIAAA. Lord Killanin also explored the attitude of the AAA officials with his friend Lord Burghley, president of the IAAF. Killanin, working within the framework of the IAAF constitution, in his discussions with the interested parties explored the possibility of merging the three Irish bodies while providing those athletes in Ireland with a British nationality with the opportunity to represent Great Britain in international competitions. He eventually proposed that the NACAI and the AAUE unite in the Republic of Ireland and be affiliated to the IAAF, and the NACAI and the AAUE merge in Northern Ireland with the affiliation remaining unchanged. A new federal body would then be created to organise All-Ireland championships, set up friendly internationals and select international teams. This proposal was acceptable to the AAUE but was rejected by the NACAI, while the NIAAA opted not to commit until the NACAI and AAUE merger took place.

In the 1960s renewed attempts to broker a deal began with Fr Kevin Ryle centrally involved. After telling the delegates to the convention of the Connacht branch of the NACAI in 1958, 'For the survival and development of athletics in this country we must have unity – unity on a federal basis if necessary. This is a matter that Irishmen, North and South, can solve if there is sufficient goodwill, tactfulness and understanding', Kyle opened contacts with personnel in the AAUE and the NIAAA and included Jack Crump (secretary of the AAA) and government minister Jack Lynch in his field of contacts. The NIAAA were unwilling to engage until such time as the NACAI recognised that it was the internationally recognised governing body for athletics in Northern Ireland and until the AAUE and the NACAI resolved their differences in the Republic of Ireland. Flags were also part of the discussion agenda. Lynch held informal meetings with officials and officers from the NIAAA and the Ulster branch of the NACAI met unsuccessfully on six occasions between 1963 and 1967.

Talks aimed at achieving agreement proceeded without NIAAA involvement, and on 18 June 1966 a crucial meeting was held in Dundalk, chaired by Judge J.C. Conroy, where a provisional agreement was negotiated between NACAI and AAUE personnel. This formed the basis for the proposals placed before the members of both the AAUE and the NACAI at two special congresses staged in Dublin in April 1967.

BORD LÚTHCHLEAS NA
HÉIREANN (BLE), 1967–1999

Sunday, 16 April 1967 is a very significant date in the history of Irish sport. On this date, delegates voted (85–33) to dissolve the NACAI at a special congress held at Jury's Hotel in Dublin; the AAUE delegates unanimously performed a similar execution in their assembly at Moran's Hotel. The two bodies were replaced by Bord Lúthchleas na hÉireann (BLE). The new body was divided into four regions with each region responsible for organising and administering athletics within its own area.

BLE was affiliated to the IAAF and fully conformed to the rules and regulations of the international federation. An executive committee of eight members from each of its two constituent organisations was formed and, pending the adoption of a constitution, this committee had plenary powers 'to promote and develop athletics and to organise matches and competitions'. The agreement achieved substantial unity in athletics for the first time since the mid-1930s and provided an opportunity for most of those engaged in athletics in the Republic of Ireland to participate in international competitions. The agreement precipitated a split in the NACAI. A minority refused to accept the verdict and the organisation continued in existence until 1999 restyled as the National Athletics and Cultural Association. In a move designed to isolate the NIAAA, competition between it and BLE and its clubs was forbidden until agreement was reached on the introduction of a 'free zone' for athletics in Northern Ireland, which would allow them to compete for Great Britain or the Republic of Ireland depending on their nationality or allegiance.

A BLE National Championship was immediately organised and Dick Hodgins became the association's first champion when he won the 15-mile road race title. In June, the first international event organised by BLE was held when Belgium, Ireland and Iceland competed in the Europa Cup match at Santry Stadium, and was televised live. The first national championships were held at Santry on 29–30 July; a separate women's championship was held at Tipperary town on 17 September 1967. The new constitution of BLE was adopted in February 1969 and its first congress was held in April. Shortly afterwards, Bord Lúthchleas Oganach na hÉireann (BLOE) was established as a subsidiary of BLE to promote juvenile athletics.

ATHLETICS ASSOCIATION OF IRELAND

On 8 November 1999, officers of BLE and NACAI assembled at the Burlington Hotel, Dublin and formally established the Athletics Association of Ireland (now Athletics Ireland/AI) as the governing body for athletics in the island of Ireland. On the previous day, delegates from BLE decided unanimously to disband and accepted a proposed unity document. Negotiations on the proposed new departure in Irish athletics had concluded in May 1999 and its terms were already accepted by the Northern Ireland Athletics Federation (NIAF). This body was established in 1989 by the amalgamation of the NIAAA and the Northern Ireland Women's AAA.

Delegates to the NACAI Congress also reluctantly accepted the proposed agreement. Michael Heery, president of the NACAI, who led the negotiation team on behalf of his organisation, had a much more difficult task in persuading delegates to support the proposals which involved the NACAI disbanding for 2 years, and the forty delegates who supported the proposed merger constituted exactly the two-thirds majority required. The agreement recognised and accepted the rights of the NIAF under IAAF rules in its membership of UK Athletics. The working relationship between the various organisations was recognised in the establishment of subcommittees with 'added support of members of the NIAF'. It was agreed that athletes from Northern Ireland were free to choose to represent either Great Britain or Ireland in the major events organised under IAAF rules. These included the Olympic Games, the World Championships, European Championships and World Cross-Country Championships. All athletes resident in Northern Ireland were declared eligible for selection for Northern Ireland in the Commonwealth Games regardless of whether they chose to represent Great Britain or Ireland in the major IAAF competitions. A transitional executive committee was formed of elected officers of BLE and NACAI to decide on an administrative structure for the new body, to draft a constitution and organise and supervise competitions. In the meantime, the constitution and rules of the IAAF were adopted by AI as its constitution and rules. A group of NACAI members formed the ACTIVE NACA, who were unhappy with the signing of the agreement prior to the new constitution being created and approved by the IAAF. At the meeting of the Council of the IAAF held at Monaco on 18–19 November 1999, the Athletics

Association of Ireland was approved and confirmed as the member for the island of Ireland.

These developments took place at a time of major restructuring of British athletics. Athletics Ireland benefited from the support of UK Athletics, a company limited by guarantee, incorporated on 16 December 1998. Prior to this, in 1991, the BAAB, the AAA and the Women's AAA (WAAA) voted to terminate their existence and the trio merged to form the British Athletics Federation. At the same time the AAA and the WAAA also merged to form the AAA of England. UK Athletics replaced the BAF in 1998.

CONCLUSION

The history section of the Athletics Ireland website informs readers, 'It is accepted the organisation [Athletics Ireland] was formed in 1873 and adopted the trading name of Athletics Ireland in 1999'. Quite clearly this is not the case and such a claim stretches the bounds of historical credibility well beyond breaking point. The pathway to the formation of Athletics Ireland was long, meandering and difficult; the sport of athletics suffered much collateral damage before the final destination was reached. Irish athletics has few rivals for the honour of being the sport most influenced by politics anywhere in the universe.

4

THE GOLDEN AGE
OF IRISH ATHLETICS
(1880–1914)

There is no real argument against the claim that the period between 1880 and 1914 provided Irish athletics with its Golden Age. Irish athletes enjoyed their most fruitful period in international competition, winning numerous titles in the Amateur Athletics Association (AAA) Championships, and assembled an impressive collection of Olympic medals. World-best marks too numerous to list were recorded by several Irish athletes across a range of events.

AAA CHAMPIONSHIPS

The AAA Championships began in 1880 and were quickly established as the world's principal athletics meeting. They were open to the world and by 1900 the list of medallists extended to five continents. Gold medals and titles were shipped to Ireland with extraordinary frequency. The Olympic Games did not develop as a credible international sporting festival until the 1908 Games were staged in London. Excluding 1900, an Irish-resident athlete won at least one AAA championship each year from 1881 to 1912; eighty-two titles were collected in eleven events, the majority in throwing and jumping events. In 1900, when the Irish returned home without a title, John Flanagan, this time representing the USA, was a comfortable winner of the hammer title. The long jump (twenty-two titles), shot-put (twenty-two) and hammer (sixteen) were Irish fiefdoms.

Pat and Maurice Davin began the trend in 1881, with Maurice emerging from retirement to compete in the championships staged at the Aston Lower Grounds in Birmingham. Pat and Maurice and a third brother, Tom, won twenty-nine Irish titles between them and all established world-best figures for their main events. Tom was the first to record a world best with a 1.78m (5' 10¼") high jump at the inaugural ICAC Championships in College Park, Dublin in 1873. In his hometown of Carrick-on-Suir, in 1880, Pat Davin recorded the world's first 1.90m (6' 2¾") high jump and in 1883 set two long-jump world-best marks of 7.06m (23' 2"). The brothers' journey to Birmingham was worthwhile: Maurice won the shot-put and hammer titles and Pat completed a long- and high-jump double. The elder Davin set two world-best marks in winning the hammer (30.124m/98' 10") and shot (12.05m/39' 6½") titles in throwing from a 7' circle. Maurice Davin dominated Irish weight throwing in the 1875–1879 period and won five successive hammer national titles after perfecting a method of throwing the wooden-handled hammer with one hand, and five shot-put titles. Tom Davin's interest in athletics tended to vary, but Pat Davin's life was consumed by the sport which he dominated in the period 1878–1883, winning five national high-jump and 120yd hurdles titles, four long-jump titles, as well as a shot-put and 100yd title. In 1884, his career was interrupted by rheumatic fever; the GAA's All-Round Championship encouraged him to return in 1886 and, watched by 30,000 spectators, he was a comfortable winner of the GAA's first multi-event title. It was his seventeenth national title, and added to this two AAA titles and three world-best marks formed a remarkable portfolio of athletic achievement.

William J.M. 'Jumbo' Barry was the second Irish hammer thrower to land the AAA title and his victory, the first of five, in 1885 began a long period of Irish dominance that ended only in 1902. During this time, fifteen of the seventeen hammer titles were won by Irish resident athletes. Apart from Barry's five, J.S. Mitchell (three) and John Flanagan (1896) became champions before emigrating to the USA and the great Tom Kiely returned to Carrick-on-Suir as champion on five occasions. These men set the international standards for their events. According to the IAAF's *Progression of IAAF World Records* Barry set eight new world-best marks, J.S. Mitchell eleven and John Flanagan fifteen as he advanced the record from 44.46m (145' 10½") to 56.18m

(184' 4") between 1895 and 1909. The contribution of Matt McGrath and Paddy Ryan to the event's history will be considered later.

In 1899, the four great stars of Irish athletics, Tom Kiely, Walter Newburn, Patrick Leahy and Denis Horgan, retained their 1898 titles and brought the total number of AAA titles won by Irish athletes past the fifty mark. Horgan won the seventh of an extraordinary thirteen AAA titles, setting a championship record (14.03m) which remained unbeaten until 1913. At the age of 41, Horgan won his thirteenth title in 1912, a record for a single event in the AAA Championships which is unlikely to be ever equalled (1893–1899, 1904–1905, 1908–1910, 1912). He was runner-up in 1900 and finished in second place in the hammer event on seven occasions between 1896 and 1909. He also established seven world-best throws for the shot-put, throwing from a 7' square, which was the practice in Ireland, extending his record from 13.79m (45' 3") in 1894 to 14.88m (48' 10") in 1904. Tipperary-native James Ryan won his second AAA high-jump title in July 1885, and on 19 August 1895 jumped 1.945m (6' 4½") to set a new world-best mark. Walter Newburn emerged as an important figure on the national stage in 1896 when he won the long-jump titles at the GAA and IAAA National Championships and his improved form in 1897 signposted the extraordinary season he enjoyed in 1898. The season began in record-breaking fashion in May 1898 when he set a new Irish long-jump record of 23' 4½" and broke Pat Davin's long-standing record in the process. In June at the Postal Sports in Dublin he jumped over 23 feet on four occasions setting a new world's best of 23' 9⅜" with his best effort. The AAA Championship provided another record-breaking opportunity and his winning leap of 23' 7" set new championship and English all-comers records that surpassed the previous best mark of the legendary C.B. Fry. On 16 July 1898, Walter Newburn finally broke the 24' long-jump barrier. In the international contest against Scotland at Ballsbridge, Newburn secured his place in athletics history with a jump of 7.33m (24' 0½").

The history of athletics is decorated with stories of personal rivalries providing the inspiration for superb individual performances. Walter Newburn's record and barrier-breaking achievements established new targets for Peter O'Connor as he was refining his technique and focusing his energies on challenging Newburn's marks. The late 1890s and early 1900s were O'Connor's period of pomp. He was born on 24 October 1872, in Millom, Cumberland, where his parents were short-term economic migrants. He is, undoubtedly, the finest all-round jumper in the history of Irish athletics. In July 1901, he became the first athlete to jump over 7.62m (25') but the effort was not officially recognised. On 5 August 1901, O'Connor jumped 7.61m (24' 11¾") to set a world record that was not surpassed until 23 July 1921. This was O'Connor's fourth world-best mark and the first world long-jump record officially recognised by the IAAF in 1912. It wasn't beaten by a British athlete until Lynn Davies jumped 7.72m in the Commonwealth Games in 1962. It remained an Irish record until Carlos O'Connell broke it on 2 June 1980. O'Connor won six successive AAA long-jump championships (1901–1906) and two high-jump titles (1903–1904). His disputes with the authorities reduced his harvest of Irish titles to five GAA titles and four IAAA championships in long, high and triple jumps. He contented himself by competing in the AAA Championships where he 'received respect, fair play and sportsmanlike treatment'.

OLYMPIC COMPETITION

This period was also the most successful for Irish athletes in Olympic competition who were either individual entrants in 1900 and 1904 or represented Great Britain and Ireland in 1906 and later. In 1906, Olympic competitors were entered by National Olympic Committees; in the earlier edition of the Games individual entries were accepted.

Pat Leahy from Creggane, County Limerick was the first Irish track-and-field athlete to experience Olympic competition when he competed in the Paris Games of 1900. Although he won two AAA high-jump titles (1898, 1899), Leahy had a reputation for not always bringing his best form with him when he travelled abroad. A brilliant high jumper, he won the GAA high-jump title in 1898 with a clearance of 1.97m (6' 5½"). He also cleared 1.95m (6' 4¾") at Millstreet, County Cork, an effort that survived as a European best until 1913. In Paris, Leahy was well short of this standard; he managed 1.78m (5' 10") in the high jump to finish in second place behind champion Irving Baxter (USA), who cleared 1.90m (6' 2"). He also qualified for the final of the long jump where a leap of 6.95m (22' 9¾") secured third place behind Alvin Kraenzlein and Meyer Prinstein, two of the great long jumpers of their generation. Leahy finished in fourth place overall in the triple jump. In winning silver and bronze medals in Paris, on 15 July, Pat Leahy became the first Irish-born competitor to be awarded Olympic medals in athletics, beating John Flanagan to the honour by a single day.

The exploits of Tom Kiely in St Louis in 1904 will be examined later in this chapter. John J. Daly also travelled to St Louis where he medalled in the steeplechase. The Daly family resided in Dowras House in Corofin, County Galway where they farmed 190 acres of land, and this allowed Daly to compete internationally from 1904 onwards. On 2 July, he travelled to Rochdale and finished in second place in the AAA steeplechase championships. He then represented Ireland against Scotland in Belfast, travelled to Queenstown and on 31 July departed aboard the *Campania* for New York, en route to St Louis to compete in the Olympic Games. The steeplechase was staged on the opening day's track-and-field programme of 29 August 1904. The runners had to clear several hurdles and a 14' water jump on each of the five laps. Daly, the only non-American in the field of seven, was the event favourite; the top American runner James Lightbody was making his debut in the event. Daly took an early lead and by the fourth lap he had opened a gap of 50m over Lightbody. Unfortunately, he faded rapidly in the final lap, and was overtaken by the USA runner who won in a time of 7:39.6 with Daly crossing the line a second later.

Three Irish athletes, Peter O' Connor, Con Leahy and Daly participated in the 1906 Intercalated Games and apparently discovered, to their dismay, that they were entered as British athletes only when they arrived in Athens. Encouraged by Richard 'Boss' Croker, *The Irish Field* organised a campaign to finance the cost of sending Irish athletes to Athens and O'Connor and Leahy were beneficiaries of this initiative. Daly self-financed his trip. The long jump in Athens brought together Peter O' Connor and Meyer Prinstein in competition for the first time. Prinstein proved superior with a best jump of 7.20m (23' 7½") to O'Connor's second-place-securing effort of 7.025m (23' ½"). The veteran O'Connor's series of jumps were well short of his personal best but his competitive instincts still throbbed and he achieved his best jump with his final attempt. O'Connor later claimed that the competition was riddled with irregularities and that biased judging had robbed him of victory. The presentation ceremony, when the national flags of the three leading jumpers were hoisted to signify the placings, provided the occasion for the first political protest in Olympic history. The tipping point for O'Connor occurred when the Union Jack was hoisted as his national flag. The incensed athlete intervened to renounce his identity as a British competitor and publicly asserted his Irish nationality. O'Connor climbed the flagpole, unfurled his green Irish flag with the words '*Erin go Bragh*' embroidered beneath the symbol of a harp and gold branch and waved it vigorously while the flag-waving Con Leahy stood guard beneath.

O'Connor recovered from his long-jump exasperations to win the triple jump and the gold medal his superb jumping career so richly deserved. Once again he produced his best jump with his last effort and secured the title with a leap of 14.075m and shunted Con Leahy to second place. The victory provided O'Connor with another opportunity to display his Irish identity. 'O'Connor', the *New York Sun* reported, 'although the British flag was hoisted when he won, walked about the stadium waving his Irish flag to show the assemblage where he hailed from.' The *Irish Independent* reported that O'Connor presented two Irish flags to Prince George and asked to have them hoisted instead of the Union Jack. This was refused, and in what the *Irish Independent* referred to as a 'stirring incident', 'all the Irishmen present produced green flags and waved them victorious in the air'.

Con Leahy balanced the demands of competing in the triple and high jump simultaneously by producing four of the five best triple jumps recorded. Both competitions were held on 30 April with the conclusion of the high jump dragging into the following day, an excruciating contest at which the opening height was set at 1.375m and was only raised by a centimetre for most of the opening day. Contestants were not allowed to pass at any height. Leahy had the consolation of winning the high jump with a leap of 1.775m (5' 10"), the lowest winning height in Olympic history and the same height cleared by his brother Pat when he finished second in 1900.

John J. Daly competed in the 5-mile race and the marathon in Athens and suffered for the cause. In the former event, Daly finished in third place and was an overnight bronze medallist. He was disqualified the following day for interference with Edward Dahl (Sweden) as the pair engaged in a head-to-head struggle down the finishing straight for third place. Daly also competed in the marathon in what was then the most international field assembled in a marathon race. After 15 miles, his feet began to blister badly and a recurrence of the old football injury reduced him to walking pace. He was forced to retire with feet that were in a terrible state. 'I never in my life saw such a pair of feet on a human. They were in a shocking condition,' Peter O'Connor recalled. Daly had great difficulty adjusting to the olive-oil and goat-based Athenian food. In a wonderful account reproduced in the *Tuam Herald* in July 1906, he explained that 'We got goat's milk, goat's butter and meat in every form from roast to devilled. It was always goat, all but horns and whiskers. I could not drink the tea served nor use any of the food, and gradually became weak.' Clearly, not the type of preparation the dieticians would recommend prior to a marathon race.

The 1908 Games were staged in London. The AAA, the Scottish AAA and the IAAA agreed that athletics entries would be for Great Britain and Ireland and representatives of the three organisations met in Manchester on 10 June 1908 and selected the team. Twenty-one Irish-based athletes (who competed in the IAAA Championships) were selected to compete in eighteen events; only in the pole vault, javelin, marathon and relay races were Irish athletes absent. Some athletes were chosen to compete in several events. Con Leahy and Tim Ahearne were selected in six events, for instance. Two days prior to the opening ceremony, twelve of these athletes represented Ireland in the international match against Scotland staged at Edinburgh on 11 July. Con Walsh, who represented Canada in the Games, was also a member of the Ireland team. In addition, seven Irish-born athletes resident in Britain competed in the track-and-field events as well as four in the tug of war. The AAA designed a circular badge that included the emblems of the four home countries in each corner for use by athletes in the track-and-field events. Irish athletes pinned this badge on to the IAAA singlets they wore in competition. These singlets featured an entwined-shamrocks logo in their design.

Three of the selected athletes won medals in 1908, the veteran shot-putter Denis Horgan, the novice triple-jumper Tim Ahearne and the defending Olympic high-jump champion Con Leahy. The venerable Horgan made his Olympic debut, at 37 years of age (born on 18 May 1871), when his best days were behind him and he had recovered from a serious head injury sustained in New York. In 1905, he moved to America and joined the New York police force. In the autumn of 1907, he was severely beaten and suffered life-threatening injuries in the course of his police duties. He survived but his injuries were such that he was pensioned from the force and returned to Ireland in March 1908, where he resumed his athletics career. His chief rival in 1908 was Ralph Rose, the greatest shot-putter of the pre-First World War era and the 1904 Olympic champion. They competed against each other for the only known time in London; Rose comfortably dealt with Horgan's challenge winning with a best effort of 14.21m (46' 7½"), almost 60cm beyond Horgan's best of 13.62m (44' 8¼").

The superb Olympic record of Irish jumpers at the Games continued in 1908. Tim Ahearne from Athea, County Limerick won the triple-jump title. In 1907 he completed a long- and triple-jump double and tied for the high-jump title at the GAA Championships before switching his allegiance to the IAAA. On 8 June 1908, he made his Dublin debut and won the long jump and the 120yd hurdles at the IAAA Championships. He represented Ireland against Scotland at Edinburgh on 11 July 1908. Two weeks later, he travelled to London and was one of twenty competitors in the Olympic triple jump, an event that rarely featured on athletics programmes. Ahearne and a Canadian from Nova Scotia, J. Garfield MacDonald, dominated the competition and both produced their best performances in their final three jumps. With his final jump, Ahearne set a new Olympic record of 14.92m (48' 11¼") to take the gold medal, with MacDonald unable to match Ahearne's effort with his final attempt. The defending champion Con Leahy was the favourite to win the high-jump title, having won four successive AAA titles from 1905 to 1908 and the American AAU title in 1907 (1.85m/6' 1"). On this occasion, Leahy finished in a three-way tie for second place with a jump of 1.88m (6' 2") and added another silver medal to his Olympic collection in what ended an athletics era.

Irish athletes representing Great Britain in track-and-field competitions were distinguished by their scarcity in Stockholm. The great days when Irish-resident athletes, and especially the freakishly talented jumpers, were world leaders in their events were over. The dominance of hurling and Gaelic football in Irish rural society, age, the damaging impact of disputes between the GAA and the IAAA, internal divisions within the GAA's athletics community as well as emigration had all taken their toll. Of the medals won by Irish-based track-and-field athletes in the 1904 and 1908 Games, only Tim Ahearne's gold was won by an athlete under 30 years of age. Ahearne and his younger brother Daniel emigrated to the USA in 1909 as did Con and Pat Leahy.

TOM KIELY: 'GREATEST ATHLETE OF IRELAND'S GREATEST ATHLETICS PERIOD'

The golden boy of Ireland's athletics Golden Age was indisputably Tom Kiely, the second eldest of a family of three boys and seven girls born to William and Mary Kiely on 25 August 1869. Kiely displayed an obsessional and incessant competitive zeal in a career that stretched over twenty-one seasons between 1888 and 1908, during which time he reportedly won an estimated 3,000 prizes, five AAA hammer titles, as well as fifty-three national titles under both the GAA (thirty-eight) and IAAA (fifteen) dispensations in running, jumping and throwing events, and an Olympic title in 1904. He represented Ireland on eight occasions between 1895 and 1903 in the international contest against Scotland in the long jump, 120yd hurdles, shot-put and hammer throw. He confirmed his versatility in this series by setting Irish (1898) and Scottish (1899) records in the hammer, and in 1895 he broke the 14-year-old Scottish long-jump record with a spectacular leap of 6.77m (22' 2½") from a grass take-off. His talents were not confined to the athletics arena. In 1896 the *Waterford News and Star* reported:

> He can take the floor and dance an Irish jig with a grace of expression that a professional might envy, and what is more can tune the fife to discourse most excellent music and has done so it may be said at many meetings where dancing competitions formed part of the programme.

Kiely made his debut as an athlete at Clonmel on 8 August 1888. In 1889 he competed in the GAA National Championships and finished runner-up in four weight events and in third place in three events. He first came to national attention on 1 August 1892 when he won the IAAA all-round title at Ballsbridge and defended it in 1893 and 1894. He won the GAA version of the event in 1898, the last occasion such a championship was hosted in Ireland. Kiely retired undefeated in all-round competitions and his domination of the Irish championships was a major factor in the ending of the event. His perfect record (six wins from six events) has been surpassed, in the twentieth century, by just a single multi-event athlete, the 1948 and 1952 Olympic decathlon champion Bob Mathias, who retired with a perfect record of eleven victories from eleven events. Prizes and titles were important to Kiely and, on the inside cover of one of his scrapbooks, he carefully documented his competitive outings and the number of prizes won on each occasion between 1888 and 1895, during which time he won 269 prizes in total (including the dancing competition at Kilmallock, County Limerick in 1893!). His most successful year was in 1893 when he won sixty-seven prizes. Based on this information, the claim that Kiely won in the region of 3,000 prizes in his career is seriously exaggerated. A figure in the region of 1,000 is a more realistic assessment based on his 1888–1895 success rate as documented in his scrapbooks.

The foundation of the Kiely legend was established in Jones' Road (later Croke Park) on 10 September 1892 with an extraordinary performance in the GAA All-Ireland Championships, when Kiely, in a feat of athletics domination unmatched in the history of Irish sport, won seven titles on the day including the long and triple jump, the 120yd hurdles and four different weight events. This virtuoso display included a magnificent triple-jump victory with an effort of 15.12m (49' 7"). Unfortunately, a serious thigh-muscle injury curtailed his jumping and he never subsequently regained the same spring and elasticity. In 1893, at Mitchelstown, he set the first of several world-best marks when he threw the 56lb weight (unlimited run and follow) 10.64m (34' 11"), beating the record of James Mitchel, and then improved on the mark at Nenagh, Kilkenny and Clonmel before the season ended.

Although he was neither a neighbour nor a relation of the Davin family, as is often claimed, Kiely's career carries the indelible stamp of the Davin influence. The Kiely residence of Ballyneale was located about 4 miles from the Davin homestead at Deerpark in Carrick-on-Suir, but it became a central place in his social world once he embarked on an athletics career. Pat Davin provided the specialist coaching to Kiely in the jumps and hurdles events and Kiely's career was in many ways a mirror image to that of Pat Davin with its emphasis on jumping, hurdles, all-round competition and weight throwing. Tom Kiely's skill in the weight-throwing events owed much to the careful training of Maurice Davin.

Tom Kiely was well past his best as an athlete when he travelled to St Louis in 1904 to contest what was advertised as the World All-Round Championship. He was approaching 35 years of age; only fourteen of his fifty-three Irish championships were won after 1899 and he had last competed in an all-round championship in 1898. He was lured out of semi-retirement by the prospect of challenging the best American athletes in a test of all-round athletic excellence and refused all offers of financial support from the AAA and from the New York Athletics Club, the Irish-American Athletics Club and the Chicago Athletics Club to represent them.

At St Louis, Kiely competed in the ten-event American Athletics Union (AAU) 'All-Around Championship', billed as the World Championship. All ten events were held on Independence Day, 4 July 1904, the traditional date for holding the competition. St Louis was hit by an all-day downpour on the day of the competition. Winds raged and the new track at Washington University was transformed into a sea of mud. The events were the 100yd, shot-put, high jump, 880yd walk, hammer throw, pole vault, 120yd hurdles, 56lb throw, long jump and 1-mile run. Scoring was based on a specialised points system that subjectively operated for the 100yd and the 120yd hurdles where only the winners were timed and the others were awarded points based on an estimate of the distance they were behind the winner.

The AAU Championship was a true test of ability in which a competitor was rewarded for his efforts in all ten events. Seven athletes competed in the championship, including Jack Holloway from Bansha, County Tipperary, an Irish pole-vault champion who competed as a member of the Greater New York Irish-American Athletics Club and finished in fourth place. Three of the last six events were Kiely specialities and he won the hammer, the hurdles and the 56lb weight throw to accumulate a final tally of 6,036 points and win the title with 129 points to spare. The *St Louis Star* acknowledged Kiely as 'undoubtedly the brightest star that the athletic firmament has ever known'. Kiely spoke of the severe test provided by the competition, a test made more difficult 'when one has to go through it in 5 hours, in the face of a blinding rainstorm, on a new clay track, soaked with water and mud and is something more than I care to go through again'.

Tom Kiely's St Louis achievement was publicly acclaimed in Ireland and he was eulogised as the 'world champion'. He returned to Ireland on 7 October 1904 to a welcoming party at Queenstown which included Maurice Davin and was led by the president of the GAA, James Nowlan, and its honorary secretary, Luke O'Toole. Kiely was welcomed as the 'living embodiment of our Gaelic manhood, as the greatest modern exponent of Irish physical culture and as the chief ornament of the Gaelic arena today'. The man himself had little time for personal adulation and his patience with the trappings of celebration had been exhausted by the time he returned to Carrick-on-Suir. On the day of his return, the town's people waited at the railway station with the brass band prepared to provide the conquering hero with an appropriate welcome. Unfortunately for the welcoming party, Tom Kiely, independent to the last, disembarked from the train at the edge of town and walked home through the fields to Ballyneale!

Official recognition as an Olympic champion was a different matter for Tom Kiely. In St Louis, he competed in the All-Around Championship of the AAU for which he was awarded a gold medal. Up to the mid-1950s, he had not been recognised as an Olympic champion. After examining Kiely's gold medal, David Guiney made contact with Hungarian historian Dr Ferenc Mezo who subsequently included Kiely as a St Louis champion in his 1956 book *The Modern Olympics*. As a result, the AAU conducted a detailed examination of the athletics events of the St Louis Games and submitted their findings to the IOC. Finally, in 1969, Tom Kiely was officially included in the list of Olympic champions at St Louis, over 65 years after the event was held and almost 20 years after the great champion's death.

5

IRELAND AND THE USA
(1900–1924)

THE IRISH WHALES

John Flanagan, Matt McGrath, James Mitchel, Pat McDonald, Martin Sheridan and Paddy Ryan won a total of twelve gold, eight silver and two bronze Olympic medals representing the USA between 1900 and 1924. These athletics behemoths, collectively known as the Irish Whales, won an amazing seventy-nine USA Amateur Athletics Union (AAU) titles in the hammer (thirty-one), 56lb weight (thirty-seven), shot-put (seven) and discus (four) events during their period of pomp. Their collection of forty-two world-best marks in standard events was equally impressive. As recorded in the IAAF's *Progression of IAAF World Records*, these were achieved by John Flanagan (twenty-two), James Mitchel (eleven), Martin Sheridan (five), Matt McGrath (three) and Paddy Ryan (one).

The origin of the collective name is uncertain. It was first used in 1914 and was popularised by the *New York Times* journalist Arthur Dailey, a writer who never allowed the facts to disturb a good story. Dailey claimed that an exasperated waiter aboard the liner taking the athletes to the 1912 Olympic Games in Stockholm, exhausted from ferrying food to the athletes, whispered, 'It's whales they are not men'. They were reputed to take five plates of soup as a starter and then demolish three or four steaks with trimmings. No doubt the name was also related to their massive size; it has also been suggested that the name was inspired by the colours of their police uniforms.

Irish emigration to the USA had become a success story by 1900. The Irish were successful in politics, business, law enforcement and sporting arenas. The New York Irish had made the transition from law breakers to law makers and enforcers. McGrath, Flanagan, Sheridan and McDonald had distinguished careers as New York policemen, but for these men entry to uniformed employment was not immediate. John Flanagan emigrated to the USA in 1896, and was in New York for 6 years before he joined the police force; Matt McGrath worked as a blacksmith, bartender and salesman between 1897 and 1902 before he too enlisted. McDonald spent a similar period in civilian life before taking up his police duties in Times Square. Martin Sheridan's career profile included time spent as an athletics instructor in the Pelham Bay Park Athletics Club. He joined the police force in January 1905 at a time when his status as an amateur athlete was under scrutiny.

Membership of the police force helped these athletes in their athletics careers. The day-to-day work schedule generated a natural level of fitness. Involvement in Police Athletics Leagues provided additional opportunities to compete. They were also compensated for loss of earnings during their time competing. In December 1913, the police commissioner was authorised to pay $2,400 in compensation to the police athletes who competed in the Olympic Games.

SCIENTIFIC TRAINING

Suggestions that these athletes were products of a vibrant Irish athletics tradition should be treated with extreme caution as the facts do not support such myth making. They were products of the New York athletics system, the most technically advanced in world athletics at the time; in addition, the north-eastern urban centres of the USA provided the most competitive athletics environment to be found anywhere. Each weekend, athletics clubs large and small joined religious, ethnic, social and political organisations in promoting well-publicised track-and-field meets. Outside of the two main clubs in New York, as many as 700 clubs catered for the athletic masses.

Immersion in this culture where excellence was appreciated and encouraged was central to the development of these champion Irish-born athletes. Pat McDonald, Martin Sheridan and, to all intents and purposes, Matt McGrath only became involved in athletics when they emigrated. The upwards trajectory of Paddy Ryan's career profile after he moved to New York is proof positive of the city's influence. A scientific approach to training was adopted, a development identified by the *Los Angeles Times* in 1908 when it reported, 'America trains her athletes as she does her race horses. Our athletics are filled with technicalities and minute points of which British athletes do not dream.' Mike Sweeney explained what was involved in this level of training as early as 1895. In preparation for the international contest against London, he secured a leave of absence from his business and went into 'active training in the way of work, diet and sleep at the summer home of the NYAC in Travers Island. The change in my routine gave me the first good opportunity of my life to devote to conditioning myself ...' The result was a new high-jump record by Sweeney in the international meet.

CELTIC PARK

New York was dotted with venues for athletics competition and the most important, Celtic Park, was developed by the Irish-American community. The guiding light behind this venture was William Prendergast who, in late 1897, purchased a dedicated home for Gaelic sports in the Laurel Hill district of Queens, close to Long Island City, for a fee of $8,000. He then formed a shareholders' group who purchased shares at $50 each and within a year recovered his initial investment. Prendergast was subsequently eased out of the consortium and the venue was controlled by members of the Greater New York Irish Athletics Association (GNYIAA) who made track-and-field events the central feature of the venue. The Celtic Park complex became the venue where athletes were nurtured and trained by the GNYIAA (founded in January 1898), which was reconstituted in 1904 as the Irish American Athletics Club (IAAC).

Celtic Park hosted fundraising events as well as social and sporting occasions for a wide spectrum of Irish and American society. The construction of a two-storey club house was completed in 1901 with facilities that included a dining room capable of seating 1,000 customers and a basement with bowling lanes. The second floor included a café, dressing rooms, a reception room and a private dining hall. On the west side, an enclosed grandstand seated 2,500 spectators who paid for the privilege of enjoying their sport in comfort.

Athletics and sports clubs were a prominent part of the New York cultural landscape with the rivalry between the IAAC and the NYAC being particularly intense. The NYAC was the club of James Mitchel and Matt McGrath, and also of John Flanagan in the early stages of his career. The IAAC challenged and eventually trumped the dominance of the NYAC. Membership of the IAAC was dominated by the Irish, but the club quickly became an ethnically diverse and socially inclusive organisation. The club was remembered by Abel Kiviat, one of the club's Jewish members, as a 'kind of a poor man's club and included policemen, firemen, sanitation workers and other laborers and school kids like myself'. The payment of travelling expenses and entry fees to competitions was a standard benefit gained from membership of a major New York athletics club. This was important given the geographic extent of the North American continent. Paddy Ryan, for instance, won AAU hammer titles in New York, Pasadena, Chicago and Philadelphia.

JAMES MITCHEL: THE ORIGINAL OF THE SPECIES

James Sarsfield Mitchel, born at Bartoose, Emly, County Tipperary on 30 January 1864, was the original and the unluckiest of the whale species, as his finest days were behind him when the Olympic Games became a festival of athletic importance. The GAA All-Ireland Athletics Championships were his personal fiefdom between 1885 and 1888 when he won seventeen national titles; he also won an IAAA shot-put title (1887). He established his international reputation at the AAA Championships, where he won three successive hammer titles (1886–1888) and two shot-put titles (1886–1887). Mitchel was one of the star members of the GAA's party of fifty-one Irish hurlers, athletes and officials who toured the north-eastern USA between late September and 31 October 1888, and was one of several athletes who chose to remain in the USA (where he dropped the second 'l' from his surname). From 1889 to 1896, he won eight successive USA hammer titles, the full sequence of 56lb weight titles from 1891 to 1897 as well as four more titles out of sequence. Mitchel extended the hammer world best from 36.40m (119' 5") set at Limerick in 1886 over eleven stages of improvement to 44.21m (145' ¾") in New York in 1892.

James Mitchel made his Olympic debut at St Louis in 1904, six months after celebrating his fortieth birthday, and won an Olympic bronze medal in the 56lb weight event where he finished just 3cm behind John Flanagan, who moved into second place with his last attempt. Ill luck dogged his final attempt at Olympic participation. On 4 April 1906, a day after departing for Athens, the liner was hit by a huge wave and several athletes were injured. James Mitchel's injury, a dislocated right shoulder, was the most serious and prevented him from competing in the stone-throwing event in Athens. Prior to John Flanagan, Mitchel was undoubtedly the greatest performer the world had seen in the weight events; he won over seventy national and regional weight-event titles in Ireland, England, Canada and the USA.

JOHN FLANAGAN: 'THE FATHER OF THE MODERN HAMMER THROW'

The career of John Flanagan epitomises the virtues of the American way. It is unlikely that he would have reached his peaks of excellence throwing a makeshift and outdated hammer around the fields of the family farm in Kilbreedy, County Limerick. Although he was an AAA champion (1896), and the holder of a world-best mark in the hammer when he emigrated, it was only when he settled in New York that the hammer became his specialist event and he became the first to master the three-turn technique.

Flanagan improved on the world best nineteen times in the pre-IAAF era, beginning with a throw of 44.46m at Clonmel on 9 September 1895 and completing the sequence with 56.19m (184' 4") at New Haven on 24 July 1909. The first of Flanagan's three successive Olympic hammer titles was secured at the discredited 1900 Games in Paris with the minimum of competitive exertion, and he won the title with a throw of 51.01m (167' 2"). He defended his title with relative comfort at St Louis in 1904 where his opening heave of 51.23m (168' 1") was the best of the day. Two days later, Flanagan's best effort of 10.16m (33' 4") in the 56lb weight throw was good enough for a silver Olympic medal. He secured his third hammer title in London in 1908 where he earned a special place in Olympic history. He became the only athlete to win three successive Olympic hammer titles, and the feat remained unique in athletics until Al Oerter won the third of his four successive discus titles in 1964. John Flanagan also regained his world record when he achieved a lifetime best of 56.18m at Newhaven, Connecticut on 24 July 1909. He fulfilled his ambition to represent Ireland after he returned to reside in Limerick. On 5 June 1911, he made his debut in the IAAA Championships winning two titles in the hammer and 56lb weight throw. This earned him international selection against Scotland, where he beat Tom Nicholson in the hammer event. On 27 May 1912, he made his final competitive appearance at the IAAA Championships at the RDS Showgrounds, Ballsbridge, Dublin and appropriately won the hammer title.

MATT MCGRATH: 'HE IS NEARLY TOO LEGENDARY TO BE TRUE'

John Flanagan's successors Matt McGrath and Paddy Ryan reached new peaks of excellence in hammer throwing. Matt McGrath was born on 28 December 1875 at Curraghmore, Burgess, County Tipperary, and emigrated to the USA in 1893. He first met John Flanagan in New York in 1906 and was introduced to hammer throwing, 'the prettiest and most skilled action' he had ever seen. After at least 13 years' residence in New York, he attracted the attention of James Mitchel who was 'generous with his advice and suggestions'. The impact of the association was almost immediate and, in 1907, McGrath won the Canadian title with a world-best throw of 52.90m.

He was little more than a novice thrower with an injury when he finished runner-up in the Olympic hammer final in 1908. On 29 October 1911, he set his second world-best hammer mark with a throw of 57.10m at Celtic Park. In 1912, in Stockholm, McGrath was the finished article and he overwhelmed the opposition with one of the all-time great Olympic field-event performances. His winning throw of 54.74m (179' 7") was 6.35m better than that of Duncan Gillis (Canada) in second place and remains the greatest winning margin in Olympic hammer-throwing history. The shortest of McGrath's throws was 4.47m ahead of Gillis' best effort and his 1912 Olympic record was not bettered until Berlin in 1936; McGrath's 1912 distance would have been good enough to win the silver medal in London in 1948!

These remarkable performances were delivered at a very difficult time in McGrath's personal and professional life. On Christmas Eve 1910, he shot George Walker, a visitor to his house, and beat him with his blackjack in the belief that he was an intruder. Walker claimed that he was invited to the family home by McGrath's wife Loretta to help dress a Christmas tree. Walker was charged with 'unlawful entry', and McGrath with assault as a result of a complaint lodged by Walker. At the trial, held in March 1911, McGrath was found not guilty. McGrath was then charged with conduct unbecoming a police officer and dismissed by Police Commissioner James Cropsey, but Rhinelander Waldo, who succeeded Cropsey, reinstated McGrath to the force. The episode had little impact on McGrath's athletics or police career. He twice received the NY Police Medal of Valor and was promoted to sergeant in 1916, lieutenant in 1918, captain in 1927, deputy inspector in 1930 and inspector in 1936.

As a 44-year-old, he was still seriously competitive in 1920 and was narrowly defeated by Paddy Ryan for the AAU title (50.68m to 51.62m). Unfortunately, McGrath suffered a knee injury in the qualifying round at the Antwerp Games and was forced to withdraw after two throws. There is no doubt the injury cost him a third Olympic hammer medal. His best throw of 46.67m, over 8m short of his 1912 effort, was still good enough to secure fifth place. McGrath again qualified for the USA team in 1924 and for the final round of throws. Amazingly, he moved from fourth in the final to second place (50.84m) to win his third Olympic medal. As a 53-year-old, in 1928, he incredibly came within an ace of becoming the only USA track-and-field athlete to compete in five Olympic Games.

MARTIN SHERIDAN'S NINE OLYMPIC MEDALS

Martin Sheridan was born in Bohola, County Mayo on 28 March 1881 and emigrated to the USA in 1899, following the trail of his brother Richard, who emigrated some years earlier. The older Sheridan was a top-flight practitioner of the throws in the USA, winning the AAU title in 1901 and 1902 and a hammer title in 1900. Martin Sheridan's introduction to athletics was accidental rather than part of any grand plan. Soon after arriving in the USA, he joined

Richard and John Flanagan at a training session in the grounds of the Pastime Athletics Club in New York. The athletes ended their session with an impromptu discus-throwing competition. When they finished, Martin Sheridan took some experimental throws and discovered to his surprise that his efforts were respectable when compared to the efforts of the two experts. On 14 September 1901, at Paterson Stadium, New Jersey, in his first meeting of significance, he set the first of what were to be five world-best marks for the discus when he threw 36.77m (120' 7¾"). He achieved his last world-best on 10 October 1909 at Celtic Park when he threw 43.54m (142' 10¼").

Sheridan made his Olympic debut at St Louis in 1904 where the giant USA shot-put expert Ralph Rose provided the surprise of the discus competition. After six throws, Rose and Sheridan were tied for first place with efforts of 39.28m (128' 10½"). On the only occasion in Olympic history, a throw-off was organised; each athlete was given three additional throws and Sheridan emerged as a comfortable winner with a best throw of 38.96m (127' 10¼"). At the Intercalated Games at Athens (1906), Sheridan was the outstanding American athlete and the most successful competitor of the Games. He competed in seven events and won two gold and three silver medals in the process. He was clearly the greatest discus thrower in the world, and he turned the final in Athens into an exhibition of discus throwing as an art form, recording Olympic best marks with two throws. In the shot-put, he took advantage of the absence of Ralph Rose and Denis Horgan to win a second title with a best effort of 13.325m.

The lack of standardisation in athletics at the time was reflected in the number of now-discontinued events featured. Sheridan won three silver medals in the stone throw, the standing long jump and the standing high jump. He also competed in the Greek-style discus throw, in which he finished in fourth place and was forced by injury to withdraw from the pentathlon, which was included in the Olympic programme for the first time. Sheridan's performances in Athens were acknowledged by a banner headline in the *New York Times*, which proclaimed 'Martin J. Sheridan, World's Greatest All-Round Athlete'. Nineteen points were scored by this wonderful man single-handed, nearly half the entire total scored by the English team and a quarter of that made by the whole American contingent. Many of the countries of Europe … failed to tally even a third of what Sheridan did alone.'

Sheridan also competed in all-round championships in which his unique combination of power, speed and agility made him unbeatable. He competed in three AAU championships in 1905, 1907 and 1909, winning each time, and set a world best on each occasion, peaking at 7,385 points, a mark which the great American-Indian athlete Jim Thorpe surpassed in 1912. He returned to the London Games of 1908 where his best throw of 40.89m (134' 2") was good enough to secure a third successive Olympic title. He completed an Olympic discus double as he also won the Greek-style title. His winning throw of 37.99m (124' 8") set a new world best and Olympic record in what was his last Olympic final. The standing jumps were still part of the Olympic programme and Sheridan's standing long jump of 3.22m (10' 7") was just good enough to scrape into third place and earn him the only bronze medal of his Olympic collection. Sheridan retired in 1911 after a decade of competition. His total of nine Olympic medals in athletics is surpassed only by Olympic immortals Ray Ewry, Paavo Nurmi and Carl Lewis.

1913: PADDY RYAN'S *ANNUS MIRABILIS* AND MORE

Paddy Ryan was born on 20 January 1883 at Bunavee, Old Pallas, County Limerick. In 1897, the 14-year-old Ryan attended the athletic sports meet at Old Pallas and returned with a new hero and a new mission in life. He witnessed Tom Kiely deliver one of his characteristic performances when he won several events on the day's programme. On the same evening, the young Ryan fashioned his own makeshift hammer and began a weight-throwing career that culminated in Antwerp with a victory in the Olympic hammer final. Ryan made remarkable progress and in 1902 won his first All-Ireland hammer title at the Markets Field in Limerick with a throw of 41.45m (136' 0") and in doing so inflicted a rare Irish defeat on his idol. He also won the unlimited run and follow hammer title again defeating Kiely. Ryan won a further ten national titles and represented Ireland twice against Scotland before he emigrated with his considerable potential unfulfilled. He 'was one to speedily turn his trainer grey-haired', according to athletics historian Bill Dooley. 'What John L. Sullivan was to boxing Ryan was in athletics, almost to the letter.'

All this changed when Ryan settled in the USA in September 1910. Unlike his fellow Irish athletes, Ryan did not join the police force but was employed as a labour foreman by the Edison Energy Supply Company; however, he did become a member of the IAAC. The competitive environment, the club dynamic, systematic training, improved equipment and endless opportunities to engage in competition and his rivalry with Matt McGrath all contributed to Ryan's metamorphosis. He progressed from third (1911) and second (1912) place finishes to win his first AAU title in 1913, at Forbes Field, Pittsburgh and then defended the title each year until his retirement in 1921, except for 1918 when he was in France with the American Expeditionary Forces, where his unit comrades included the future world heavyweight boxing champion, Gene Tunney. On his return journey to the USA, he visited Ireland and won the IAAA hammer and 28lb weight throwing titles.

Paddy Ryan was ineligible to represent the USA at the 1912 Olympic Games as he had yet to obtain USA citizenship; his form in 1913, Ryan's *annus mirabilis*, indicates an opportunity missed. Apart from winning his first AAU title, he set the first officially recognised IAAF world record for the hammer when he threw 57.77m (189' 6½") on 17 August while competing at the Eccentric Fireman's Annual Handicap Games at Celtic Park, New York. The record survived until 1938 and remained as an American record until 1953. Before the year ended he established four world-best marks in non-standard weight events.

Personal rivalries between athletes who challenge the conventional boundaries of their events is a central part of athletics history. In the 1910s, the rivalry of Matt McGrath and Ryan dominated the hammer event. The pair battled throughout the decade at distances that were far ahead of their contemporaries and those that came later. Celtic Park showcased much of the best of what the men had to offer. This was the venue where McGrath threw a world best of 57.10m (187' 4") on 29 October 1911 and where Ryan established the first officially recognised world record. Between them they won fifteen of the nineteen AAU hammer titles between 1908 and 1926 with Ryan winning eight to McGrath's seven. The 1920 Olympic hammer competition was held on 18 August 1920 and was expected to be a showdown between Ryan and McGrath, the two senior citizens of the event. McGrath's knee injury forced his retirement after two throws and, in his absence, Paddy Ryan had an easy victory: his best throw of 52.874m was 4.445m ahead of Carl Lind (Sweden) in second place.

PAT MCDONALD: THE 'BABE' FROM DOONBEG

Pat McDonald was the shot-put specialist of the group. McDonald was born in Killard, County Clare, on 27 July 1878 and moved to the USA in 1901 where his job as a traffic policeman at the junction of 43rd Street and Broadway, Times Square, New York between 1905 and 1920 made him the city's most famous policeman. Inspired by the feats of John Flanagan and Martin Sheridan, he joined the IAAC and, after experimenting with discus and hammer throwing, he switched to the shot and enjoyed remarkable success. In the absence of the great Ralph Rose, he won the AAU title in 1911 and retained the title in 1912, beating Rose, who was unquestionably the greatest shot-put exponent of the era. The pair had no serious rivals for the 1912 Olympic title. In the qualifying rounds, Rose in his opening throw set a new Olympic record of 14.98m and extended this to 15.25m with his third effort to easily lead the qualifying phase, with McDonald's best of 14.78m almost 0.5m behind. In the first round of the final, McDonald produced a lifetime best of 15.34m and set a new Olympic record that survived until 1928. Rose was unable to improve on his qualifying mark and was relegated to the silver-medal position. McDonald also won a silver medal in the shot-put-with-both-hands competition on the only occasion the event was held in an Olympic Games. In this event, the best left-handed put and the best right-handed put were added to produce an athlete's total. The gold medal was snatched from McDonald's grasp by Ralph Rose when his last throw elevated him from third to first place.

McDonald, the fifth Irish-born competitor to win an Olympic athletics medal representing the USA, continued to compete with remarkable success after the Stockholm Games. He won the shot and the 56lb weight event at the AAU Championships in 1914, 1919 and 1920 and represented the USA at both events in the 1920 Games, where he also enjoyed the privilege of carrying the USA flag at the opening ceremony. In Antwerp, McDonald was restricted by a hand injury and was relegated to fourth place during the final series of throws. There was, however, gold-medal consolation for McDonald in the 56lb weight throw, an event that was restored to the Olympic programme after an absence of 16 years. Three Irish athletes – McDonald, McGrath and Paddy Ryan – were selected to represent the USA in the event, but the knee injury incurred in the hammer competition forced McGrath, the favourite, to withdraw. In a closely contested final, McDonald held the lead from the qualifying round from Paddy Ryan and maintained it to add a second gold medal to his Olympic collection. McDonald was selected as an honorary member of the USA team in 1924 and was again honoured with the privilege of carrying the USA flag in the opening ceremony with the USA name standard carried by Matt McGrath.

PAT FLYNN OF BALLINADEE, COUNTY CORK

With the exception of Pat Flynn, top-quality Irish middle-distance runners of Olympic medal-winning standard resident in the USA were a rarity during this era. Flynn was born in Ballinadee near Bandon, County Cork on 19 December 1894 and prior to emigrating he won the IAAA 4-mile championship in 1913 and was a most impressive winner in the same event for Ireland against Scotland at Celtic Park, Belfast on 19 July 1913. He emigrated in September 1913 and as Sergeant Pat Flynn served in the Rainbow Division of the USA Army during the First World War in France. He resumed his athletics career on returning to New York and as a member of the Paulist Athletics Club won the AAU steeplechase title in 1920 with a new USA record (9:58.2). This championship doubled as the Olympic trial and the victory earned Flynn his place on the USA team for the 1920 Games. In Antwerp, the steeplechase final was dominated by Percy Hodge (Great Britain) who took control after the first lap. Flynn finished an estimated 21 seconds behind Hodge in second place.

AGE WAS NO BARRIER

These Irish-born athletes enjoyed athletics careers of extraordinary longevity. James Mitchel made his Olympic debut as a 40-year-old veteran; Matt McGrath was approaching 33 years of age when he first stepped into the Olympic throwing circle in 1908 and almost 49 when he stepped out for the last time in 1924. McGrath has one of the longest careers at the highest level of any track-and-field athlete. He finished in second place in the hammer throw in 1907 in the AAU Championships and last competed in the event in 1928 where he finished in fifth place at 52 years of age. John Flanagan was 43 years old when he first had the honour of representing Ireland in an international contest against Scotland in 1911 and last threw the hammer competitively at the IAAA Championships in May 1912.

Age-related records established by these athletes include:

- Matt McGrath, at the age of 49 years and 195 days, in Paris in 1924 became and remains the oldest competitor, medallist and finalist in Olympic track-and-field history.
- Pat McDonald, at 42 years and 26 days, in Antwerp in 1920 is the oldest person to have won an Olympic track-and-field gold medal.
- John Flanagan is the oldest hammer gold medallist in Olympic history. He was 40 years and 168 days old when he won his third hammer title in London on 14 July 1908. Flanagan is also the only hammer thrower to have won three successive Olympic titles.
- John Flanagan set his last world-best hammer-throw mark of 56.20m (184' 4½") at 41 years and 196 days, the oldest world-record breaker in track-and-field history.
- Paddy Ryan is the only Irish-born athlete to set an IAAF recognised world record in a weight event with his throw of 57.77m (189' 6") made in New York on 17 August 1913.

GREAT NON-OLYMPIC MEDALLISTS

Others too made a significant impact on the world of athletics without achieving Olympic fame. Mike Sweeney was one such athlete. He was born on a small farm outside Kenmare, County Kerry in 1872 and grew up in Canal Street, New York. He was introduced to athletics as an 18-year-old when he joined the Xavier Club and within a year he had broken the world record for the high jump when he cleared 1.95m (6' 5") at Travers Island, New York. Sweeney raised the world best on three more occasions in 1895, his best effort made in a match between New York AC and London AC staged in New York when he cleared the bar at 1.97m (6' 5⅝) on 21 September 1895. Sweeney was declared a professional athlete when he was employed as a sports coach at the Hill School near Philadelphia and as a result his athletics career was limited to competing in professional events.

The exploits of Clane-born Thomas Conneff are detailed later. Daniel Ahearn, the younger brother of 1908 Olympic triple-jump champion Timothy, emigrated to the USA in 1908 and won the AAU triple-jump title on eight occasions (1910–1911, 1913–1918). On 30 May 1911, he jumped 15.52m (50' 11") at Celtic Park, New York and this effort was recognised by the IAAF as the first official triple-jump world record. He was ineligible to represent the USA in the 1912 Olympic Games and was past his considerable best when he competed in Antwerp in 1920, where he finished in sixth place (14.08m).

6

IRELAND, THE EMPIRE AND THE UNITED KINGDOM

BOBBY KERR: SPRINT GOLD IN LONDON 1908

Bobby Kerr, born in Coolatrain, near Florencecourt, County Fermanagh on 9 June 1882, became the only Irish-born Olympic sprint medallist when he finished in third place in the 100m and won the 200m in London in 1908. The family emigrated to Canada in 1889 and settled in the industrial city of Hamilton. Bobby Kerr competed in the St Louis Games without making any impression and was unable to finance a trip to Athens in 1906. In 1907, he won the Canadian 100yd and 220yd titles, set a Canadian record of 9.4 seconds for the 100yd and was selected to represent Canada at the London Games.

A letter sent from London to his sister Diana provides a fascinating insight into Bobby Kerr's personality and his London experiences. Kerr was impressed by London 'although the traffic was something awful'. The king 'is a fine looking old gentleman, the Queen is all painted up'. He was 'surprised by the English people' and changed his perceptions of them. There were some 'fine people' in London; 'we only get the scum in Canada', he wrote. As a strict teetotaller, he was less impressed by their drinking habits. 'The drink is awful, not only the men, but the whole family go in ...' Bobby Kerr was a devout Methodist and while in London 'generally' attended service twice on a Sunday. He attended the City Road Chapel, 'the home of Methodism where John and Charles Wesley preached', and also worshipped at the City Temple where 'Rev Joseph Parker once preached'.

Kerr warmed up for the Olympics by competing in the AAA Championships at the Olympic Stadium in Shepherd's Bush ('a wonderful place capable of holding 100,000 people'), where he won the sprint double and was awarded the Harvey Gold Cup as the outstanding athlete of the championships. The three favourites qualified for the 100m Olympic final: Kerr, Reggie Walker and James Rector (USA). A poor start in the final destroyed Kerr's chances. After a duel with Rector, Walker went ahead about 20m from the end and won by a stride with Rector just holding on to second place, inches ahead of the fast-finishing Kerr. Kerr had a second opportunity to win a sprint gold and he qualified for the 200m final with victories in the opening heat in an Olympic record of 22.2 seconds, and in the semi-final (22.6). In the final, Kerr benefited from a flying start, established a significant lead at the 150m stage and held on to win a rare track gold for Canada (22.6). Back in Hamilton, the bells, led by the massive bell in the James' Street City Hall, rang out to alert the residents of Kerr's victory. Kerr visited his native Fermanagh after his Olympic duties ended.

Bobbie Kerr returned to England in 1909 to defend his AAA titles and finished second in the 100yd and third in the 220yd on 3 and 4 July. Members of the Tiger Amateur Athletics Association organised the Bobby Kerr Benefit held in Britannia Park, Hamilton on 15 May 1909 to help fund his trip to London and over 2,500 Hamiltonians attended to support their hero. Kerr also fulfilled an athletics ambition on this trip as he represented Ireland in the international match against Scotland and duly delivered a victorious 100–220yd double.

FROM CARRIGANIMA TO CANADA AND BEYOND

Con Walsh, a native of Carriganima, a village located halfway between Macroom and Millstreet, County Cork finished in third place in the 1908 hammer final with a throw of 48.51m (159' 1½") behind John Flanagan and Matt McGrath. Walsh was an interesting inclusion on the Canadian team as he had a rather tenuous connection with Canada at this time and his considerable portfolio of athletic achievement was accumulated mainly in an Irish context. Throwing the 56lb weight was his speciality; he was also a Gaelic footballer of note. His athletics party piece at this time was in kicking a Gaelic football long distances and he won three All-Ireland GAA titles in the discipline in 1901, 1905 and 1906 with a national-record effort of 64.72m (212' 4"). He cut an ungainly figure in his initial forays into the hammer-throwing arena. Tom Leahy, one of the famous jumping brothers, observed the Carriganima giant's awkwardness and advised him to practise step dancing 'so that he could put his feet where he'd want them'. The advice was taken and, in the 1906 GAA Championships, Walsh won national titles at three versions of throwing the 56lb weight in addition to the hammer title.

Con Walsh emigrated in April 1907 and won the Canadian AAA hammer title (46.94m). His Canadian base at this time was in Woodstock, Ontario. Canada provided Walsh with a convenient ticket of opportunity to compete in the Olympic Games and he won the hammer event at the Canadian Olympic trials. However, the Canadian Olympic Committee refused to fund Walsh for the London Games and instead elected to send an additional track runner. Walsh did not travel to the Games with the main body of Canadian team members. Neither did he stay with them at their quarters at 65 Sinclair Road in Kensington or appear in the stadium team picture taken prior to the Games, nor did he march with the thirty-two-member Canadian contingent in the opening ceremony.

Three days prior to competing in London (11 July 1908), Walsh represented Ireland against Scotland at Edinburgh where he won the hammer event with a throw of 49.56m (162' 7"), at the time, the best throw recorded on Scottish soil. He then travelled to London and on 14 July represented Canada in the Olympic Games, where he easily qualified for the hammer finals with a throw of 48.51m (159' 1½"). He was unable to improve on this with his final three throws when faced with the intimidating might of John Flanagan and Matt McGrath, and had to settle for the bronze-medal position. He returned to Ireland after the Olympic final and competed for Ireland against the USA at Ballsbridge on 1 August 1908, he then travelled south and competed at a number of athletics meets in Munster before returning to the USA.

He won the USA 56lb weight throw title in 1910, and then shocked McGrath to win the USA hammer title in 1911 at Forbes Field, Pittsburgh, with a personal best and championship record of 54.12m (177' 6½"). Having finally established himself as the world's best hammer thrower, Con Walsh retired.

KENNEDY MCARTHUR: MARATHON OLYMPIC CHAMPION

Kennedy Kane McArthur, born in Dervock, County Antrim on 10 February 1881, was one of South Africa's earliest sporting heroes. McArthur is the only Irish-born winner of the Olympic marathon and at 1.88m (6' 3") and 77kg (170lb) is also the tallest and heaviest winner.

He emigrated to Potchefstroom, South Africa in early 1901 and became a volunteer member of the Baden-Powell South African Constabulary, a special police force created to administer law and order in the Transvaal and Orange River Colony during the last 2 years of the Boer War (1899–1902). In South Africa, as a member of the Johannesburg Harriers and Athletics Club and later the Pretoria Harriers, he developed into an international-class runner, particularly after switching from middle distance and cross-country to long-distance running. He progressed through the ranks, first winning local races and later provincial ones, and then found his niche as an international-class marathon runner.

In April 1908, Kennedy McArthur made a spectacular entrance into the South African élite athletics scene and from that date until July 1912 he remained unbeaten in the six 'marathon' races he contested. These included the South African Olympic trial race in 1908: a poor time (3:18:27.4), athletics politics and the belief that Charles Hefferon was a better all-round runner led to McArthur's non-selection for London. In 1911, McArthur set South African 10-mile (52:46.2) and 5-mile (25:34.4) records as he sharpened his speed on the track and, in April 1912, he won his first national track title, the 10 miles (55:11.2) at the South African Championships at Cape Town. The team for the Stockholm Games was announced after the meet and departed for London the following Friday. This was the last occasion when South Africa saw the great McArthur in serious action as his running career ended after the Olympic Games.

McArthur was granted special leave of absence, without pay, of 114 days from 10 May to 31 August 1912 to enable him compete in Stockholm. The South African team arrived in Southampton on 27 April 1912 and moved to a base in Brighton. The underfunded team was dogged by financial difficulties in Stockholm and became known as the 'the Bread and Milk' team. The only uniform the athletes received was a headband and a jacket with an emblem on the pocket. The athletes were also provided with dark green, silk athletics clothes with gold trim, which McArthur wore in the marathon race.

The Stockholm marathon was the first held on an out-and-back course at the Olympic Games. It started and finished in the Olympic Stadium and was raced on a flat 40.2km course watched by 'tens of thousands of spectators along the route'. After the problems in London in 1908, no 'minders' were allowed, 'each man being left to his own devices, no attendants with refreshments were allowed and all benefited'. Instead race officials manned refreshment stands located at 500m intervals along the route where water and refreshments that included tea, coffee, oranges and lemons were available. The reported race-day temperature of 32°C in the shade provided McArthur and his teammate Christopher Gitsham with a considerable advantage. The European athletes raced in an uncomfortable heatwave that was normal for McArthur and Gitsham. Potchefstroom, where McArthur lived and trained, had summer temperatures that regularly oscillated between 30 and 35°C. McArthur, without his knowledge, also carried another in-built advantage with him to Stockholm. He was the first successful athlete to benefit from high-altitude living. Potchefstroom is situated at 1,400m above sea level and today it is a popular high-altitude place of training for international athletes.

At the halfway stage, Gitsham led by 10 seconds from Finland's Tatu Kolehmainen (1:12:40) with McArthur (1:13:15) in third place. The Finn dropped out at the 35km stage, McArthur joined his teammate at this point and the South African pair led the field by over a minute. The result hinged on a crucial incident about 2 miles from the finish. At the base of a hill, Gitsham stopped to take a drink of water at a roadside fountain but McArthur pushed on (he took no refreshments throughout the race) and established a winning lead. The giant marathon runner won by just under a minute from an enraged Gitsham, in a time of 2:36:54.8. McArthur's most anxious moment happened about 50m from the finish when a massive laurel wreath 'tied with long streamers of Swedish blue and yellow' was draped over his shoulders, causing him to stumble. No country has since produced the first two finishers in an Olympic men's marathon.

Kennedy McArthur was catapulted to international stardom. On the evening of the race, a reported 4,000 people sat down, under electric lights, for a banquet in the stadium at which McArthur was the most honoured guest. The prize-giving ceremony, conducted by King Gustav V, was held a week later. McArthur received the gold medal, a certificate, an oak wreath and the bronze statue of Pheidippides. He became a superstar in Stockholm and was mobbed by adoring female fans, whose number included Princess Maria of Sweden. He then travelled to his native Dervock where he was greeted with another round of acclamation. Huge crowds gathered at Ballymoney Railway Station to salute the conquering hero on his arrival. The men of the town unhitched the horses from the carriage sent for him, and pulled it through the Union Jack bedecked streets to a civic reception in the Town Hall. He was presented with an address in the form of an album of miniature paintings of his native county. He was then taken on the short trip to Dervock where he was greeted by a candlelit procession and reunited with his parents and family.

On the return journey to South Africa, an honorary dinner was given by 'a few English athletes' for McArthur on 16 August 1912 at Pinoli's Restaurant in London. He arrived back in South Africa on 3 September 1912 to an unprecedented welcome in Potchefstroom 'where on no previous occasion, not even excepting the Royal visit, had there been such a spontaneous outburst of enthusiasm'. In December 1913, he ran a 10-mile race in Potchefstroom and this proved to be his last race. A foot injury caused by a fall from his bicycle while on police duty never healed properly and ended his running career. The Potchefstroom Town Council later decided to present Kennedy McArthur with a plot of land on which he built a house, and in the early 1920s he belatedly received a small cash presentation that had been collected as a testimonial immediately after his 1912 victory.

TUG-OF-WAR: EDWARD BARRETT – ALONE HE STANDS

Tug-of-war was part of the Olympic programme in the early Olympic Games and was a popular inclusion in athletics programmes in the late 1800s and early 1900s. It was particularly popular with police forces and a number of Irish-born policemen won Olympic medals competing for Great Britain in 1908 and 1912. In the 1908 Olympic tug-of-war final, the London City Police Team defeated the Liverpool Police. Four Irishmen earned Olympic tug-of-war medals in this final.

Edward Barrett, a member of the London City Police, was the gold-medal winner. Barrett emigrated in 1902 from Rahela, Ballyduff, County Kerry, and joined the London police force in 1905. He was an outstanding and versatile sportsman who excelled at sports that required power and technique. He joined the GAA in London and was a member of the London team that won the 1901 All-Ireland hurling title (played on 2 August 1903 at Maurice Davin's field in Carrick-on-Suir, County Tipperary), and when he won an Olympic gold medal in 1908 he achieved a unique distinction in Irish sport and one that will never be equalled. He is the only All-Ireland hurling medal winner to have also won an Olympic gold medal (or indeed a medal of any colour). The British heavyweight freestyle wrestling title winner in 1907, Barrett also won a bronze Olympic medal in the heavyweight category in freestyle wrestling in 1908. Edward Barrett is worthy of a place at any table of Ireland's greatest all-round sportsmen. His All-Ireland hurling medal, his Olympic gold and bronze medals, his British wrestling title and his multi-event participation at the London Games established Barrett's status as one of Ireland's most versatile and successful sportsmen. Apart from his tug-of-war and freestyle wrestling successes, he also competed in the discus and shot-put at the London Games. In the latter event, he finished in fifth place with his first and only effort. Another competitor dropped his shot on Barrett's ankle prior to the second round of throws and he was forced to withdraw.

Edward Barrett's brother James, a Tipperary-based RIC man, also competed in the 1908 Olympics in the shot and discus without distinction. Jim Clarke from Bohola, County Mayo and a first cousin of Martin Sheridan, Thomas Butler from Waterford city, and Patrick Philbin who was born in Skeagh, Castlebar, County Mayo on 4 August 1874, were members of the defeated Liverpool Police Team and earned Olympic silver medals.

In 1909, London policeman Mathias Hynes from Gortmore, Killanin, County Galway replaced Edward Barrett on the London City Police tug-of-war team and represented Great Britain at the 1912 Games in Stockholm where only two teams took part in the event. In the opening pull, Sweden slowly pulled the British team over; in the second pull, some members of the British team sat down for better leverage and after a number of warnings the team was disqualified. Mathias Hynes's silver medal was the fifth and last tug-of-war medal won by Irish-born competitors in the 1908 and 1912 Games.

MCGEOUGH AND HEGARTY

John McGeough was born on 20 January 1881 at the family residence in Castle Street, Armagh, the son of Thomas McGeough, a bootmaker. He emigrated to Glasgow as a young man, found employment as a postman, joined the Bellahouston Harriers and developed into a top quality middle-distance runner. He was the dominant figure in Scottish middle-distance running in the 1900s. Included in his list of Scottish title successes were six successive mile titles won between 1902 and 1907 and a seventh title in 1910. On 20 June 1903, at the Ibrox Stadium, he won the Scottish 4- and 1-mile titles as well as the 880yd in a single afternoon's work. He also successfully raided the Irish championship scene, winning the GAA 2- and 4-mile championships in 1905 and secured the IAAA 1-mile title in 1907. He represented Scotland against Ireland on nine occasions between 1902 and 1910 at distances from 880yd to 4 miles, winning on six occasions; in 1907, he was selected for both countries.

McGeough won the silver medal in the 1,500m at Athens in 1906, where he was beaten into second place by the reigning Olympic champion James Lightbody (USA). The American and McGeough were in fourth and seventh place respectively entering the final lap with McGeough apparently unaware of Lightbody's finishing speed. The American took the lead with 200m remaining and sprinted to the line. McGeough closed just as rapidly but finished 0.6 seconds behind the title holder.

McGeough acted as a trainer of Celtic FC during his time in Glasgow. In 1910, he left the city and moved to Manchester where he was employed in a similar capacity with Manchester City FC. He later returned to Monaghan where he was a founding member of the Blackhill Emerald GAA Club in 1916. The club name acknowledged his Scottish past. He resided in the Blackhill district of Glasgow where the local Emerald pipe band entertained the working classes. McGeough was involved with Cavan senior football teams as physical trainer and masseur, at different stages between 1927 and 1949. His reputation as a sports masseur and football trainer placed heavy demands on his services, with footballers and greyhounds benefiting from his gifted healing hands. He acted as trainer and masseur to the great Cavan Gaelic Football Team in the 1940s and accompanied the team to New York as masseur in 1947, on the only occasion the All-Ireland football final was played outside of Ireland.

The only Derry City man to win an Olympic medal did so at Antwerp in 1920. Anton Hegarty was a member of the Great Britain cross-country team that finished in the silver-medal position behind Finland. Hegarty's talent for running was discovered when he joined the Royal Inniskilling Fusiliers shortly after leaving school. He won Irish cross-country titles before his running career was interrupted by the outbreak of the First World War, in which he was wounded and discharged 'as medically unfit for further action'. He returned to athletics and was a founder member of the City of Derry Athletics Club in 1919. In 1920, he finished in second place in the resumed All-Ireland Cross-Country Championships and represented Ireland in the International Championships at Belvoir Park, Belfast.

He comfortably qualified for the British team in the cross-country event at the Olympic trials. The Olympic cross-country race was held over a distance of 8,000m with results in the individual race counting towards team totals. Each nation was entitled to enter six runners in the individual race with the leading three finishers of each team counted towards the team total. Hegarty finished in fifth place in the individual race, 42 seconds behind the great winner Paavo Nurmi (27:15) and was the second scoring member of the British team.

Larry Cummins from Kinsale, County Cork was also a member of the Great Britain team. Cummins emigrated in 1910 and also fought in the First World War. He finished in twenty-sixth place overall but was a non-scoring member of the silver-medal-winning Great Britain team. It is unclear whether Cummins received a medal for this performance as neither the IAAF rules nor the Olympic Charter cover the matter.

7

THE OLYMPIC MEDALLISTS

On 6 July 1924, high jumper and legendary Gaelic footballer Larry Stanley became the first athlete to represent independent Ireland in an Olympic athletics competition. He is one of 189 athletes to have achieved this standard of excellence. Dr Pat O'Callaghan, Bob Tisdall and Ronnie Delany have won Olympic titles, John Treacy and Sonia O'Sullivan are silver medallists and Rob Heffernan is the sole athletics bronze medallist. Eamonn Fitzgerald, John Lawlor, Eamonn Coghlan (twice), Sonia O'Sullivan and Thomas Barr have finished just outside the medal position in fourth place.

DR PAT O'CALLAGHAN: DUAL OLYMPIC CHAMPION

Dr Pat O'Callaghan was born on 28 January 1906 at Knockaneroe, Derrygallon about 4 miles from Kanturk, County Cork. After completing his secondary education, O'Callaghan entered the Royal College of Surgeons in Ireland (RCSI), at 16 years of age, and graduated in 1926 at the age of 20, one of the youngest graduates in the history of Irish medicine.

O'Callaghan had never seen the hammer until he arrived in Dublin. On his return to Kanturk for the summer holidays of 1925, O'Callaghan designed a makeshift hammer. He acquired cannonballs from Macroom Castle and with the help of the village blacksmith attached some steel wire to the balls and manufactured a few functional implements. The making of an Olympic champion was underway. Back home in Cork, O'Callaghan dedicated the summer of 1926 to perfecting his throwing technique. He was largely self-taught but he benefited from the advice of Garda Superintendent Denis Carey (a sixth-place finisher in the 1912 Olympic hammer competition). 'Dinny was a man of high intelligence and he impressed me on the importance of a fundamental idea in that you must never lose contact with the ground when turning in the circle,' he recalled in an interview conducted by Tom O'Riordan in the *Irish Runner Yearbook* in 1982.

O'Callaghan first competed in a high-profile Dublin athletics meet on 25 June 1927 when he won the hammer event at the Garda Sports at Croke Park with an unremarkable throw of 41.49m (136' 1½"). This was the first time O'Callaghan threw the standard-length hammer. He arrived at Croke Park without his homemade implement. Prior to throwing, he picked up several hammers and found that they were all too long. He then realised that his home-produced hammer was short of the standard length! O'Callaghan won his first Irish title in 1927 and represented Ireland in the triangular international match with England and Scotland at Manchester the same year. In 1928, O'Callaghan emerged as a significantly improved athlete and was consistently throwing over 50m, a distance that always won an Olympic medal in the past; he established a new personal best of 52.32m (171' 8") at Kanturk prior to leaving for Amsterdam. Despite his progress, O'Callaghan travelled to Amsterdam as a virtual novice in international competition: he returned as Ireland's first Olympic champion after a spectacular and surprise win in the hammer event on 30 July.

The sixteen hammer throwers in Amsterdam were divided into two groups with the top six throwers qualifying for the final sequence of three throws. O'Callaghan qualified for the final in third place overall with his first throw of the competition. In the final, with his second-last throw, the Kanturk man whipped the 16lb ball and chain out to 51.39m (168' 7") to win Ireland's first Olympic title. He was the only athlete of the leading three qualifiers to improve on his efforts in the final round.

During the competition, O'Callaghan noticed that the hammer used by the Swedish thrower Ossian Skiöld was aerodynamically more efficient than his own model. He approached Skiöld and requested permission to use the Swede's hammer as the rules of the time allowed.

Skiöld refused but O'Callaghan was supplied with the hammer after the intervention of the referee for the competition. This was the hammer thrown by O'Callaghan for the winning throw.

O'Callaghan enhanced his reputation as an international-class athlete of great all-round ability in the post-Amsterdam Olympiad. His greatest domestic success came at the 1931 NACAI Championships when he won six titles, the high jump, the hammer, shot-put, discus, the 56lb over the bar and the 56lb without follow, in an extraordinary display of athletic talent that has only been surpassed by Tom Kiely. At a 2-day international meet at Stockholm in June 1931, he won the hammer competition on both days throwing a personal best of 54.47m (178' 8½") on the second day. In August 1931, O'Callaghan recorded another personal best when he threw 56.04m (183' 10") at the Clonmel Garda Sports. This brought him to the top of the world rankings after being ranked twelfth in 1929 and third in 1930. His season's best in 1932, prior to the Olympics, an unspectacular 52.27m, also topped the world rankings.

In Los Angeles, the hammer competition was staged on 1 August at the same time as the 400m hurdles. Dr Pat O'Callaghan landed a second Olympic title for Ireland when he became the only athletics champion from 1928 to defend a title. Fourteen throwers contested the event with the top six after three throws qualifying for an additional three attempts. The story of O'Callaghan's difficulty in the Olympic final is well known. The throwing circle in the stadium was covered in hardened cinder and unfortunately O'Callaghan's steel spikes were more suited to grass and clay-covered circles. In Los Angeles, he used special case-hardened steel spikes purchased on one of his visits to Sweden. He brought three sets to Los Angeles and all three were unfit for purpose. Unable to turn with his customary speed, he struggled to produce his best. Despite the difficulty, his second throw of 52.21m was good enough to place him in second place as he picked up the hammer for his final throw. In between throws, a hacksaw and file borrowed from the ground staff were used to cut back the length of the spikes. Fate, in the form of the 400m hurdles final, intervened and the last series of throws were postponed. Immediately after his victory, Bob Tisdall became aware of his colleague's emergency and joined O'Callaghan and assisted in the filing operation. Great sportsmen confirm their greatness on great occasions and O'Callaghan, under immense pressure added almost 1.7m to his seasonal best and produced a dramatic winning throw of 53.92m (176' 11") with his final effort to relegate the 1920 Olympic shot-put champion Frans Pörhölä to second place.

Dr Pat O'Callaghan was deprived of the chance to win a third successive hammer title by the decision of the Irish Olympic Council not to compete at the 1936 Games in Berlin. This was at a stage in his career when he was throwing better than ever. He won the AAU (USA) title in 1933 (49.16m/161' 3⅜") and the AAA title in 1934 (51.43m/168' 8¾"). On 22 August 1937, he produced his best-ever throw of 59.55m (198' 8⅞") at the Cork County Championships (NACAI) at Fermoy but as the NACAI was suspended from IAAF membership the throw was never ratified as a world record, although it exceeded Paddy Ryan's mark. Pat O'Callaghan was just 30 years of age, a mere youth in hammer-throwing terms, at the time of the Berlin Games. Longevity was the order of the day amongst hammer throwers of the era; the average age of the first six throwers at the inaugural European Championships of 1934 was 36.

BOB TISDALL: 1932 OLYMPIC 400M HURDLES CHAMPION

Robert Morton Newburgh 'Bob' Tisdall was born in Nuwara Eliya in Ceylon on 16 May 1907, where his father William, a native of Bantry, County Cork, managed a tea plantation. His mother Margaret 'Meta' Morton was a native of Summerhill, Nenagh, County Tipperary, where Bob returned to receive his initial schooling before attending public schools in England. A Cambridge graduate, he was elected president of the Cambridge University Athletics Club for the 1930–1931 season and, in March 1931, in the varsity match with Oxford, he performed what the *Irish Times* described as 'one of the most amazing feats ever accomplished at any athletics meeting'. In the space of 40 minutes, he won four of the eight events in the annual contest, the 120yd hurdles (15.5 seconds), the shot-put (12.40m/40' 8"), the long jump (7.02m/23' ½") and the 440yd (51 seconds) as he led Cambridge to victory.

In April 1932, he contacted Eoin O'Duffy, the president of both the NACAI and the Irish Olympic Council, and asked to be considered for the 400m hurdles at Los Angeles. He had only once previously contested the event, during Cambridge University's tour of Greece. Much that has been written about Tisdall's success at Los Angeles has been done from the perspective that this letter was his first contact with the Irish athletics community but, at this stage of his career, Tisdall had a history of involvement in Irish athletics and was already provisionally selected for the Games in the 110m hurdles and the 400m. The novelty lay in the request to be considered for the 400m hurdles. He competed in the NACAI National Championships in 1930 where he was an impressive winner of the 120yd hurdles and was just beaten in the 440yd flat by P.C. Moore, both athletes breaking 50 seconds in the final. O'Duffy supported the request and Tisdall in his third race in the event reached the time standard set by the NACAI officials and was selected for the Games.

The journey to Los Angeles was a difficult one but the Irish Olympic Council made the wise decision to travel early to the Games to allow the athletes time to recover and acclimatise prior to competing. In 1934 Tisdall published *Young Athlete*, a book that included his reminiscences of his Los Angeles experiences. He lost weight and slept badly on the trip across the United States and his lack of experience over the 400m hurdles caused him some anxiety. He began to practise on arrival but to his horror his weight loss continued and he 'had not enough strength to finish the course'. His response amazed his fellow athletes and shocked the tough American coaches. He opted for rest and sleep, trusted his ability 'to stride the hurdles evenly when the time came' and placed 'more reliance upon skill and experience than upon mere physical strength'. Tisdall spent 15 hours a day in bed and for 8 days refused to put on running shoes or to 'run a yard'. Three days prior to his race, he began to run gently in his bare feet on the grass. This unorthodox approach, combined with Tommy Maloney's 'wonderful method of massage', using a mixture of olive oil and *poitín*, ensured that Tisdall walked on to the track for the first heat of his event 'so full of energy that even to remain walking was a restraint'.

Tisdall raced to a comfortable win in a time of 54.8 seconds in his first-round heat and 2 hours later, in his semi-final victory, he equalled the new Olympic record (52.8), set minutes earlier by Glenn Hardin (USA). This performance was extraordinary as he visibly slowed after clearing the second-last flight of hurdles and, long before Usain Bolt invented the technique, he jogged to the finishing tape. The Olympic final was held at 3.45 p.m. on Monday, 1 August 1932. Tisdall prepared meticulously in the hours before the race and horrified the traditionalists by drinking copious amounts of water to ensure that he was properly hydrated. Tisdall raced superbly and, as he approached the final hurdle, he held a lead of about 5yd from Lord Burghley, Morgan Taylor and Hardin. A slight lapse in concentration almost proved costly. Tisdall clattered the crossbar of the hurdle with his leading left leg but this had very little impact on his momentum; his trailing leg was unhindered. He still crossed the line a comfortable winner, in a new world-record time of 51.7 seconds, with Hardin second (51.9) and F. Morgan Taylor in third place (52). Under the rules of the day, Tisdall's world and Olympic record and the first sub-52 seconds in the event's history was not allowed as he had knocked a hurdle in the course of the race.

Eoin O'Duffy proclaimed Tisdall's victory 'the grandest feat ever achieved by an Irishman'. There is some substance to the claim. The final featured four athletes who secured the title during their careers: Morgan Taylor (1924), David Lord Burghley (1928), Tisdall (1932) and Glen Hardin (1936). His time was faster than Glen Hardin's winning time in 1936 and would have been good enough to win silver in London (1948), bronze in Helsinki (1952) and secure a tie for fourth place in Melbourne. Hardin never subsequently lost a 400m hurdles race; Lord Burghley ran the fastest time of his career in the Olympic final and Morgan Taylor equalled his career-best time. It would be 51 years and 312 days before an Irish hurdler ran faster. His time of 51.7 seconds remained beyond the reach of an Irish athlete until 8 July 1984, when J.J. Barry finally ran 51.56. The extraordinary Tisdall also competed in the decathlon in Los Angeles and finished in eighth place overall, the best-ever performance by an Irish athlete in Olympic competition.

The Olympic champion was unable to obtain permanent employment in Ireland; he subsequently moved to South Africa and later lived in Zambia, Kenya and Tanzania before eventually settling in Nambour, in Queensland, Australia. On 16 June 2000, Tisdall was part of Australia's Olympic Torch Relay. At the age of 93, as the oldest surviving Olympic champion, he jogged 500m as he carried the Olympic Torch into the Nambour Showgrounds. He died on 27 July 2004, at the age of 97 years and 72 days.

1956 MELBOURNE: RONNIE DELANY, IRELAND'S ONLY OLYMPIC TRACK CHAMPION

Ronald Michael 'Ronnie' Delany was born on 6 March 1935 at the family home of Hillview, Ferrybank, Arklow, County Wicklow. Shortly after the outbreak of the Second World War, the Delany family moved to Sandymount, Dublin. As a teenager in this middle-class Dublin suburb and as a pupil at the Catholic University School (CUS), Delany sampled several sports before concentrating on athletics. At the CUS Delany's potential was recognised by maths teacher Jack Sweeney, the great Irish athletics coach of the day, and, encouraged by Sweeney, the teenage Delany gradually began to concentrate on middle-distance running and especially the 880yd. He worked with Sweeney on tactical awareness and fine-tuned the 'kicking' technique that was so important throughout his career, as Sweeney emphasised the importance of making one decisive move at the crucial moment of a race.

Delany's pursuit of athletic greatness was total and included a decision to resign from an Irish Army cadetship in December 1953 as he discovered that military training was not conducive to achieving athletic excellence. Instead of the permanent pensionable status-enhancing career of an Irish Army officer, Delany opted for employment as a door-to-door salesman of domestic appliances for the Electrolux Company in Carlow and Kilkenny. He successfully sold vacuum cleaners at night and engaged in near full-time training during the day. The impact of the dedicated regime was apparent in the summer of 1954 as the Irish 880yd/800m record book was rewritten by the travelling salesman. Delany, the athlete, and Jumbo Elliott, the coach of Villanova University, discovered each other and in September 1954, in one of the defining moments of Irish athletics, Ronnie Delany enrolled in the college on a full athletics scholarship. Soon after his arrival two additions, cross-country and indoor running, were made to the Delany athletics portfolio.

Jumbo Elliott identified Delany's potential to be a great miler and in September 1955, when Delany returned to Villanova, he was advised by Jumbo Elliott 'to eat, drink and sleep the mile' with the Melbourne Olympic 1,500m title as the objective. Jumbo's assessment was correct. In January 1956, at the Boston Gardens, he began a streak of thirty-four straight indoor-mile victories that stretched over 4 years. At Compton, California, on 1 June 1956, 10 months after his first race over the distance, he became the seventh athlete to break the 4-minute barrier for the mile and the following day he set a new national record for the 880yd of 1:49.5, the first occasion an Irish runner had broken 1:50 for the distance.

He then returned to Dublin and two injury-induced indifferent performances placed his Olympic selection in jeopardy. Injured in an 800m race in Paris in early July, he made an ill-timed return to serious competition in early August. On 10 August, at Lansdowne Road in the feature-event mile, Delany finished 75yd and 14 seconds adrift of Brian Hewson in 4:20, his slowest time ever.

It is one of the enduring myths associated with Delany's victory in Melbourne that he was selected by a single vote and that this was the casting vote of the Olympic Council's president, Lord Killanin. This is total fantasy: Lord Killanin was not present at the meeting held on 3 October 1956 when Delany was selected on an 8–5 vote of those present on the night. Delany returned to Villanova and was assured by Jumbo Elliott that with 2 months' training it was still possible to win the Olympic title. Delany's autumn training, designed and monitored by Elliott was his toughest yet and, with a singular mindset, he lived the life of a recluse as he completed his two-workouts-a-day schedule. He departed for Melbourne in peak condition mentally and physically.

The thirty-seven athletes who entered for the 1,500m event in Melbourne formed the strongest field ever assembled for the event. Roger Bannister, in running the first sub-4-minute mile, had liberated athletic potential. Eighteen entrants in the 1,500m had run faster than the Olympic record set by Josef Barthel in 1952 and nine were faster than the world record as it stood prior to the Helsinki Games. The world 1,500m record was lowered six times by six different athletes over the course of the Olympiad and of these athletes, only the suspended Wes Santee was absent from Melbourne. Qualification for the final for Delany was 'a mere formality' as he eased himself across the finishing line in third place (3:47.7) behind Mervyn Lincoln (Australia) and Ken Wood (GB). He was one of five of the world's ten sub-4-minute milers who qualified for the final (John Landy, Brian Hewson, Gunnar Nielsen and László Tábori).

The fastest field in the history of the event, including the world mile-record holder and Australian superstar John Landy, assembled for the final at the Melbourne Cricket Ground on 1 December 1956. In the most important day of his career, Delany executed the perfect tactical race. Murray Halberg led the field through the first lap (58.4 seconds) but when Mervyn Lincoln took the lead at the end of the second lap, the pace sharpened. At this stage, Ronnie Delany was in eleventh place, with John Landy the last man running. The final lap began (with the bell ringer forgetting to ring the bell in his excitement) with the athletes bunched together in an 8yd space, the ideal scenario from Delany's perspective. Lincoln and Brian Hewson held the lead but Lincoln began to fade. Ronnie Delany was boxed in at tenth place but retained his composure although there were only 300m left in the race. As they moved down the back straight for the last time, Brian Hewson was beginning to extend his lead. Suddenly John Landy bolted for home and Delany reacted immediately and ran in his wake as they passed several runners who were beginning to struggle. Delany successively passed Hewson, Landy and Lincoln until only Klaus Richtzenhain (Germany) was ahead of him. Despite the stress of the occasion, Delany's tactical antennae were sensitive and delivered with perfect timing the final decisive move that secured victory.

One of the cardinal philosophies of Jack Sweeney's coaching in CUS was that an athlete should 'make one dynamic move in a race'. Delany used this tactic from the beginning of his athletics career and this occasion was no different. About 150m from the finish, he was exactly where he planned to be, on the shoulder of the lead athlete, in the 1,500m Olympic final. He switched to overdrive and sprinted for the line. The power of his sprint destroyed the field and the race was effectively over. Ronnie Delany won the 1,500m Olympic title with 3m to spare in the new Olympic record time of 3:41.2 with Richtzenhain second (3:42) and John Landy in third place (also 3:42). Despite running on the outside, Delany covered the last lap in 53.8, the final 200m in 25.6 and the last 100m in 12.9 seconds. He immediately fell to his knees in prayer and gave thanks to God for the gift he had been given. The image of Delany on his knees in prayer with John Landy standing over him is one of the great iconic images of Ireland's Olympic history.

The finishing times of the finalists confirmed the quality of the field and the event. The first eight finishers broke the official Olympic record (3:45.1) with Ken Wood, in ninth place, also breaking the record. Athletics historian Bert Nelson described the final as the greatest 1,500m race of all time.

> The winner was 0.6 seconds off the world record, an amazingly fast time under the conditions of a big, tightly packed field and the intense competition and pressure of an Olympic final. Seven men finished within 1.8 seconds of the victor, the last of them running a time which would have tied the world record 2 years ago. Competition was of the keenest, drama and tension were always present and the issue was in doubt until the very last stages ... Delany's finish was certainly the best in history.

Roger Bannister's verdict also provided the seal of approval to Delany's performance: 'I never saw a more beautifully judged race.'

Ronnie Delany remains the only Irish athlete to win an Olympic title in a track event.

2000 SYDNEY: SONIA O'SULLIVAN OLYMPIC SILVER MEDALLIST AT 5,000 ...

Sonia O'Sullivan's Games began at the opening ceremony when she carried the Irish flag at the Parade of Nations. Following the Atlanta disappointment, O'Sullivan had restructured her career guided by a new coach, Alan Storey. In Sydney she comfortably qualified for the 5,000m final and, on 25 September 2000, secured the Olympic medal her glorious career so richly deserved. The 5,000m was the last of the finals held on an evening that is generally considered to be the finest in athletics history and provided a fitting conclusion to the evening's sport with drama, excitement and athleticism to equal anything that went before. O'Sullivan's main rival in the final was Romania athlete Gabriela Szabo, the 1997 and 1999 world champion who in 1999 became the first track-and-field athlete to win more than $1 million in prize money in a single year. Ethiopians Gete Wami and Ayelech Worku held the season-best times.

The early stages of the race were slow and cautious and at one stage memories of Atlanta were recalled as O'Sullivan drifted back through the pack until she was 40m adrift in tenth place. However, by the 3,000m stage she regained contact with the lead group and was a contender. Szabo took the lead 600m from the finish with Wami in second place and Sonia in third place. At the bell, Szabo sprinted for the line and O'Sullivan responded. The duelling Europeans produced one of the great races in the history of the event as O'Sullivan reached Szabo's shoulder on the backstretch but was unable to overtake the diminutive Romanian (5' 2" and 6½ stone). Sonia made repeated attempts to overtake down the homestretch but somehow, as Vincent Hogan wrote in the *Irish Independent*, 'Szabo found the strength of a lion in the frame of a small bird' and won the gold in the new Olympic record time of 14:40.79 to O'Sullivan's personal best and new Irish record of 14:41.02. Sonia O'Sullivan remains the only Irishwoman to win an Olympic medal in athletics. Later in the week, she finished in sixth place in the 10,000m final in a new Irish record time of 30:53.37.

JOHN TREACY: SILVER MEDAL ON HIS MARATHON DEBUT IN 1984

John Treacy was born on 4 June 1957 in Villierstown, County Waterford, a small village located about 5 miles from Cappoquin. Treacy attended St Anne's Secondary School in Cappoquin and the folklore that he ran home from school each evening is only partly true. In his Leaving Certificate year, he did run home from school each evening but not by the direct route, which only covered 5 miles.

At this stage, he was a member of St Nicholas AC in Ring, County Waterford. Treacy achieved success in schools' and junior athletics (he had two third places to his credit in the World Junior Cross-Country Championships in 1974 and 1975 and was a silver medallist at the 5,000m in the European Junior Championships).

Providence College, Rhode Island, was Treacy's college of choice from the many who sought the Villierstown athlete. Treacy thrived in the USA and was transformed from a very good international-standard junior athlete to a world-class senior athlete. In his last season at Providence College, Treacy captured the imagination of the Irish sporting public with a superb victory in the World Cross-Country Championships in Glasgow. He defended the title in heroic fashion in 1979 in the highly pressurised atmosphere at Limerick, where at least 25,000 attended expecting him to deliver.

In 1980 in Moscow Treacy sensationally collapsed in the final lap of his 10,000m heat as he was on the verge of qualifying for the final. His recovery to qualify for the final of the 5,000m was remarkable: he ran superbly to finish in seventh place, just 1.7 seconds away from a medal place.

In 1983, John Treacy, unhappy with his form, returned to his old athletics environment in Providence, Rhode Island and resumed the life of a full-time athlete. He linked up with cardiologist Dr Dario Herrera, a marathon fanatic who devised a training programme for Treacy and offered advice on nutrition, stretching and strengthening exercises, reading his own body and mental preparation. Treacy was regularly tested at the University of Pittsburgh by exercise physiologist Lee Cunningham, to monitor his progress. The scientific analysis pointed Treacy towards the marathon and, by April 1984, the decision was made to contest the event.

The men's Olympic marathon was the final event of the 1984 athletics programme and assembled the finest field in the history of the event. Seven starters had broken 2:09:00 for the distance; another nine had covered the distance in less than 2:10:00. World champion, the apparently indestructible Rob de Castella, was the pre-race favourite and was unbeaten in the distance since 1980. Japanese star Toshihiko Seko was also unbeaten in the five marathons he raced since April 1979. Alberto Salazar, the Boston Marathon winner and USA record holder, was in the field as was Juma Ikanga, the Commonwealth Games champion. In contrast John Treacy was making his debut in the event.

Treacy ran superbly and with Carlos Lopes and Charlie Spedding dominated the final 6 miles of the race. An injection of pace at the 35km stage by Lopes effectively ended the race for gold and Treacy and Spedding engaged in a battle for the silver, which Treacy secured with a 67-second last lap to complete his marathon debut in a time of 2:09:56.

LONDON 2012: ROB HEFFERNAN SCORES BRONZE ... EVENTUALLY

Rob Heffernan's performances in the 20km and 50km at the London Olympic Games of 2012 were magnificent in an event in which the Irish walkers delivered master classes in achieving seasonal and personal bests on the biggest stage of all. Rob Heffernan used the

20km as a warm-up event and completed the distance in 1:20:18, the second fastest time of his career to finish in ninth place in what he described as a 'very strong training session'.

Heffernan's initial fourth place in the 50km in London was a fantastic result: he smashed the Irish record in what was the finest performance by an Irish walker in Olympic competition. His race plan worked to near perfection. He distanced himself from the early blistering pace and settled for a position just outside the top ten for the first 35km. After 20km, he was 49 seconds behind the lead group of ten walkers. Heffernan shared the work with Li Jianbo (China) and with 15km remaining he increased the tempo and moved from tenth to fifth place 5km from the finish. During this surge, Heffernan gained 44 seconds on the long-time leader Si Tianfeng who dropped back to third place. However, the Chinese walker retained his third place and as Heffernan raced up the Mall for the last time, he inched past Sergey Bakulin (Russia) and moved into fourth place. Heffernan's time of 3:37:54 was a brilliant 7 minutes 36 seconds inside his previous best and the Irish national record but almost 2 minutes behind the winner Sergey Kirdyapkin (3:35:59). Heffernan's time would have won the silver medal in Beijing and the gold at every Games before that but, on this occasion, it was 38 seconds adrift of the bronze medal position.

Heffernan's performance and result was better than was realised at the time. In January 2015, winner Sergey Kirdyapkin, a dual world champion (2005, 2009), was selectively suspended by the Russian Anti-Doping Agency (RUSADA) in a manner that enabled him to retain his Olympic gold medal. He was handed a 3-year, 2-month suspension backdated to October 2012 and a selective suspension to cover the period from 11 April 2012 to 11 June 2012.

The IAAF successfully appealed this decision to CAS and Rob Heffernan was upgraded to the bronze-medal position and became the sixth athlete to medal in Olympic competition representing Ireland. On 3 November 2016, Rob was presented with his London 2012 Olympic Bronze Medal in the Concert Hall, City Hall, Cork in a special ceremony hosted by the Lord Mayor of Cork, Des Cahill. On the first occasion an Olympic medal was presented on Irish soil, Acting President of the Olympic Council of Ireland William O'Brien made the presentation.

8

THE WORLD AND EUROPEAN CHAMPIONSHIPS

1983 HELSINKI: EAMONN COGHLAN WORLD 5,000M CHAMPION

The inaugural World Championships staged in Helsinki in 1983 attracted a global TV audience of over a billion viewers. The decision to stage the World Championships was made at the IAAF's Congress at Puerto Rico in 1978, a time when boycotts were a fact of Olympic life. Primo Nebiolo, a powerful and controversial figure who played an instrumental role in bringing money and corporate sponsorship to athletics, became president of the IAAF in 1981 and immediately declared 1983 the Year of Athletics. The IAAF and the organising committee paid the travel expenses and accommodation costs of all competitors and team officials for the championships and as a result 1,355 athletes from 153 countries competed in Helsinki.

Eamonn Coghlan travelled to Helsinki with a copy of Dr Denis Waitley's *The Winner's Edge* tucked into his carry-on luggage and his mind filled with positive thoughts. At the time, an athlete was responsible for his own mental preparation and after the disappointment of successive fourth-place finishes at the Montreal and Moscow Olympic Games, Coghlan was on a mission of personal redemption. He safely negotiated the heats and semi-final of the 5,000m and qualified for the gold-medal race with the minimum of fuss. The leading runners of the time, Marcus Ryffel, Thomas Wessinghage, Wodajo Bulti, Werner Schildhauer and Doug Padilla, awaited in the final.

Coghlan was the man with the plan on the starting line. He had broken the race into three sections: in the first half he intended to conserve energy and remain towards the back of the field and then with six laps remaining to move through the field in preparation for the last stage when he 'was going to be a miler again', in the belief that nobody was capable of beating him over the distance.

The final proved to be an absorbing race with the runners reaching 1,600m in 4:26:00, an ideal pace for a pack liberally sprinkled with fast-finishing kickers. Coghlan relaxed in the back third of the pack, careful to avoid any potential trouble. The 4,000m stage was passed in 11:03.26, a perfect pace for Coghlan. Three laps from the finish, the miler's mode was activated as Dmitriy Dmitriyev made his significant move and began to sprint away from the field. Wessinghage was unable to maintain an interest and as Dmitriyev led by 20m Coghlan gave chase. Running the last lap in 58 seconds, he made his decisive move on the final bend and when he drew level with the Russian, he clenched his fists with delight, looked over at his rival a couple of times and raced clear in the final straight to become the first winner of the world 5,000m title in a time of 13:28.53, ahead of Werner Schildhauer in second place (13:30.20). In the words of BBC commentator David Coleman, Coghlan's race was 'brilliantly run ... the champion of the world ... Coghlan got it all right ... he didn't panic then, he waited and waited because once he realised that Wessinghage had nothing left, he got to Dmitriyev's shoulder very, very quickly when Dmitriyev had a long way to go ...'

Back in Dublin, U2 topped the bill for the first time in their home city at a concert billed as *A Day at the Races* at the Phoenix Park Racecourse. Bono briefly interrupted the band's War Tour to announce that Eamonn Coghlan was the champion of the world.

1995 GÖTEBORG: SONIA O'SULLIVAN WORLD CHAMPION

Sonia O'Sullivan's serious preparation for her 1995 season began in Australia in January; her second week of training involved running 105 miles 'plus a couple of track sessions and a weights session'. She returned to Teddington (London) for the spring and prepared for the track season. In the lead-in to Göteborg, Sonia raced in Moscow,

Tallinn, Cork, Gateshead, Dublin, Nice, Oslo and Crystal Palace accumulating a catalogue of victories that formed the greatest season of the greatest career of any Irish athlete. 'The summer unravels like a game of cat and mouse', she wrote in her autobiography *Sonia*. 'All the top runners watching one another, seeing who is going well, trying to work out which races they will enter in Göteborg, trying to get a little psychological edge.' The shadow boxing concluded when O'Sullivan and Fernanda Ribeiro, the two main contenders for the 5,000m world title, faced off at Crystal Palace: Sonia, the European 3,000m champion; Ribeiro, the European 10,000m champion. Sonia's mission was to scare Ribeiro away from the World Championship 5,000m; Fernanda had a similar intention and announced a planned attack on the world record for the Crystal Palace race. Sonia gained the psychological edge with a victory in 14:47.64, the fifth fastest time in history. The edge was short-lived as Ribeiro retaliated by going to Hechtel in Belgium a few days later and setting a new world record (14:36.45) for the distance.

The women's 5,000m was included in the World Championship programme for the first time. The Chinese athletes chose to forego participation in the 1995 championships for whatever reason. Sonia O'Sullivan travelled to Göteborg with a simple plan to win gold regardless of the pace of the final, held on 12 August 1995. This was just as well as Gabriela Szabo (Romania) opened with a blistering lap of 65.28 seconds and continued at world-record pace for the opening four laps. Szabo, the world junior champion, failed to crack the field and Paula Radcliffe, Ribeiro (the 10,000m title winner earlier in the week) and O'Sullivan tracked the tiny Romanian. The pace slowed and Paula Radcliffe, still searching for her ideal event, led the field through 3,000m (8:58.20) with ten athletes still interested in the race. Sonia O'Sullivan was seldom outside of second place. Ribeiro shadowed O'Sullivan and made her big move three laps from the end. O'Sullivan reacted immediately and was at the Portuguese athlete's shoulder at the bell. Sonia's crucial move came 200m from the finish and in a few strides the race was effectively over. A final 200m sprint in 28.81 seconds took Ireland's track queen to a comfortable victory in a championship record time of 14:46.7 and secured the gold medal and one of the ruby-red Mercedes E-Class cars on offer to the world champion in each event.

In *Sonia*, O'Sullivan explained that after her previous championship encounters she decided 'to keep on going, working harder and harder, getting a bit faster all the time, always working harder. I wanted to be the best. To get the best from myself. That's why I had done it all. A little slot with my name engraved in the history books.' And after Göteborg, she kept on racing and carved her name indelibly on the record books. Four days later, O'Sullivan raced in Zurich and then in Cologne, Brussels, Crystal Palace, Berlin, Rieti (Italy), Rome, Monte Carlo, Tokyo and Johannesburg. Post-Göteborg, Sonia was unbeaten and unbeatable and in a season of twenty-two races lost just once, in a 1,500m event in Gateshead where Kelly Holmes proved superior. Her Berlin victory over Ribeiro earned a pile of gold bars awarded to athletes who won at each of the Golden 4 Super Grand Prix meets. Her winning time of 14:41.30 was the third fastest in history and brought her season's record against Ribeiro to 4–0. She was honoured as the IAAF's Woman Athlete of the Year and adorned the cover of the January 1996 edition of *Track and Field News*. She was also selected as the sport's bible's Women's Athlete of the Year. The magazine's forty-five-member international panel nominated O'Sullivan by the largest margin in 5 years; twenty-five of the judges awarded Sonia their No. 1 vote. She was also the magazine's first ever No. 1 in the 1,500, 3,000 and 5,000m events in a season.

2009 BERLIN: OLIVE LOUGHNANE WORLD CHAMPION – EVENTUALLY

Olive Loughnane competed in the World 20km walk event for the fifth occasion in Berlin. Apart from a disqualification in 2005, she always finished inside the top twenty. In the Beijing Olympics, Loughnane was the fastest over the second half of the 20km race without the reward of a medal. She was determined that this would not happen on this occasion.

Loughnane had been self-coached from 2004 to 2008 and after Beijing linked up with Spanish coach Montserrat Pastor in Guadix, who worked on the athlete's technique and recalibrated her training by slowing down her 'steady stuff' and making her fast work faster. The result was apparent in the 31°C heat of Berlin as Loughnane, the oldest athlete in the field, zipped up and down the 2km loop on the Unter den Linden Boulevard, concentrating on the process involved in the technically demanding event.

The Russian Olympic gold medallist and reigning world champion, Olga Kaniskina, pushed ahead 30 minutes into the race and split the field in the process. After 10km, Kaniskina had opened a 20-second gap over Kjersti Platzer (Norway) and Anisya Kirdyapkina (Russia) with Loughnane at the front of the second group, in fifth place, 33 seconds down. Platzer and Kirdyapkina faded and Hong Liu (China) moved up to second place. Loughnane gave chase and passed her after 14km and the pair then engaged in a duel in the sun with the silver medal at stake. The duel was decided in Loughnane's favour in the final lap as the Loughrea Athletics Club athlete pulled away and finished 12 seconds ahead of Lu in a seasonal best time of 1:28.58 and 49 seconds behind Kaniskina (1:28:09).

In January 2015, Olga Kaniskina was one of five athletes suspended by RUSADA with the suspensions dated from October 2012. The already retired Kaniskina was suspended for a period of 3 years and 2 months and her results between 15 July 2009 and 16 September 2009, as well as between 30 July 2011 and 8 November 2011, were annulled. The ban was based on irregularities discovered in the athlete's biological passport, which tracks blood values over time to identify evidence of doping. Kaniskina's disqualification included two World Championship victories in 2009 and 2011. Olive Loughnane was therefore awarded the 2009 title and on 6 July 2016 finally received the gold medal in a formal presentation ceremony headed by IAAF President Sebastian Coe. 'Amhrán na bhFiann' was played and the tricolour was raised at the European Athletics Championships in Amsterdam.

2003 PARIS: GILLIAN O' SULLIVAN WALKS TO SILVER

Gillian O'Sullivan joined her namesake Sonia in Ireland's World Championship medal-winning pantheon when she finished in second place in the 20km walk in Paris on 24 August 2003 behind Russia's 37-year-old Yelena Nikolayeva, who won in a championship-best time of 1:26:52. O'Sullivan's time was 1:27:34. Nikolayeva led O'Sullivan and Elisabetta Perrone (Italy) by 20 seconds at the halfway mark; the intense heat took its toll and several athletes retired, including the defending world champion Olimpiada Ivanova. Athletes' concentration also wavered in the conditions and Chinese medal hopeful Hongjuan

Song was one of seven athletes disqualified during the race. Nikolayeva thrived in the heat; she steadily increased her lead and was 48 seconds ahead of O'Sullivan with 5km remaining, while Russia's Tatyana Gudkova moved into third as Perrone dropped out.

O'Sullivan, who finished in tenth place in Sydney in 2000 and in fourth place at the European Championships in 2002, was the medal pathfinder for élite Irish walkers who prepared the way for the later championship successes of Olive Loughnane and Rob Heffernan. O'Sullivan is also the only Irish walker to have set a world record. This was achieved in Santry Stadium on 13 July 2002 in the 10km walk, when she won the Irish title in a time of 20:02.6, a record that survives to the present day and is likely to do so for the foreseeable future as in 2004 the distance was removed from the list of events for which world records are officially recognised.

2013 MOSCOW: ROB HEFFERNAN WORLD CHAMPION

In 2011, a year after he finished in fourth place in both the 20km and 50km walk events at the European Championships in Barcelona, Rob Heffernan was forced to withdraw from the 2011 World Championships in Daegu after the sudden death of his mother. Heffernan briefly considered retiring from his sport at the end of his 2012 season but opted to continue and took on the additional responsibility of coaching Brendan Boyce and Luke Hickey. An important change was also made in his support network as his wife Marian became his manager-coach. After an 'absolute shocker' in his first serious race of 2013 in Lugano, Switzerland in a World Grand Prix race, the walker and his group spent 3 weeks training at high altitude in Morocco and this was followed by an official Irish training camp in Almeria and a summer camp in Guadix in Spain, where Heffernan completed the hardest training sessions of his life. He returned to Ireland and set a new national record of 11:11 for the 3km walk at the Cork City Sports. The final piece of the preparation jigsaw was completed in Salzburg, Austria where the essential tapering was finished immediately prior to moving to Moscow.

The 50km walk in Moscow was Rob Heffernan's first race over the distance since the London Olympics and, as he tells us in *Walk Tall*, as he warmed-up for the race, 'the nerves began to churn my stomach and within minutes I was retching and puked my guts up ... and in a strange way the puking made me realise that I was ready for the race'. An early warning card from a Polish judge had no impact; work with a Spanish sports psychologist during the summer had given Heffernan five different cues to work on and these provided focus points throughout the race. He remained close to the front and, even in the cautious opening kilometres, he never dropped outside the top ten, as the young Russian pair of Ivan Noskov and Mikhail Ryzhov pulled clear. Australian Jared Tallent and French veteran Yohan Diniz gave chase and the lead quartet became a quintet at the halfway stage when Heffernan joined the group. He maintained his composure and rhythm and shared the lead with Noskov and Ryzhov with 16km remaining. It became a two-man shoot-out for the title when Noskov was dropped, and with precisely 10km remaining Heffernan made his decisive move and pulled clear. Ryzhov was unable to maintain the challenge and the Irish athlete never looked in danger of relinquishing the lead in the closing stages. Heffernan entered the Luzhniki Stadium alone and absorbed the acclaim of the crowd for the final lap of the stadium, before crossing the line in a time of 3:37:56, which took him 68 seconds clear of Ryzhov in second place. In a remarkable coincidence, Heffernan's victory on 14 August 2013 came on the thirtieth anniversary of Eamonn Coghlan's first World Championship title in 1983.

HELSINKI 1994: SONIA O'SULLIVAN IRELAND'S FIRST EUROPEAN CHAMPION

It is somewhat of a surprise that the great Irish male athletes all failed to secure a European track or field title in the championships that were first held in Turin in 1934, when Ireland withdrew from the competition as their representation was confined to the territory of the Irish Free State. The only Irish man to have won a title, Limerick-born Jim Hogan, who represented Ireland in the 1964 Olympic Games, won the 1966 marathon in Budapest, wearing the singlet of Great Britain. Irish athletes have won three gold, six silver and four bronze medals in Europe. In the 1,500m, Ronnie Delany finished in third place in 1958, while Frank Murphy (1969) and Eamonn Coghlan (1978) were silver medallists. On 10 August 1994, Sonia O'Sullivan exorcised the deficit when she won the 3,000m title. 'What unfolded was beautiful, like a dream come true, as we watched history being created with a performance which deserves to be put alongside the great Irish sporting achievements,' Tom O'Riordan wrote in *Irish Runner*. Sonia displayed no evidence of any post-Chinese traumatic syndrome in her 1994 season. She set a new 2,000m world record in Edinburgh and a week later smashed the 10-year-old European record for 3,000m at Crystal Palace with a time of 8:21.64, the fastest non-Chinese time in history. Sonia also ran the fastest times in the 1,500, the mile, 2,000m, 3,000m and the second fastest 5,000m.

After a hectic season, she suffered three successive defeats prior to the Helsinki Championships and arrived in Helsinki as a tired athlete. Sonia and Yvonne Murray were the dominant European forces over the distance and the pair qualified for the final with obvious ease. Murray was the reigning champion, having won the title in Split when O'Sullivan finished in eleventh place on her debut in a major athletics championship.

Anita Philpott also qualified for the 3,000m final and she took the field through the opening lap (69.94 seconds). Murray had no chance of outsprinting Sonia at the finish and took on the race at this stage. She was closely shadowed by O'Sullivan and with three laps remaining the pair shared a 30m lead which had doubled with two laps to go. Sonia was patient and remained at a tired Murray's shoulder until 200m from the finish when she accelerated to the front and became the first Irish athlete to win a European title. Her control of the race was reflected in the time differential. Her winning time of 8:31.84 was more than 4 seconds faster than Murray's 8:36.48. Sonia O'Sullivan had delivered the perfect race as she won her first major championship title.

STUTTGART 1993: SONIA O'SULLIVAN WORLD SILVER MEDALLIST IN 1,500M

Sonia O'Sullivan travelled to the 1993 World Championships as a hot favourite to win the 3,000m title. Her status as the leading runner over the distance was confirmed at the Bislett Games in Oslo in July with a superb winning run of 8:28.74, a new personal best and the fastest by any athlete since the Seoul Olympics. Conventional wisdom suggested the Chinese athletes would be a minor factor in the event; conventional wisdom has seldom been more incorrect. As *Track and Field News* reported, 'They were the only factor. They grabbed this race by the neck and shook it until it offered no more fight. They ran away from the heretofore-undefeated O'Sullivan and made it look like child's play. In a mere 8½ minutes, they changed the face of women's distance running.' Five of the six medals of the 3,000m and 10,000m had been salvaged by the athletes of Ma's Army, a term that recognised the contribution of Ma Junren to their success. Junren coached eighteen female athletes in Liaoning Province in north-east China. Junren, a strict disciplinarian, claimed the success was based on a combination of an intense training regime, his bans on long hair and dating, and a diet that included the consumption of exotic potions of caterpillar fungus, soft-cell turtle soup and powdered seahorse. Ma explained that his runners were chosen from rural areas and as such were used to enduring hardships. The athletes were taken to a national training centre in Tibet five or six times annually where an intense mix of speed and aerobic altitude training including running a daily marathon was part of the programme. Junren also claimed to have perfected the science of peaking exactly after high-altitude training.

O'Sullivan recovered from her fourth-place 3,000m finish (a tactical error destroyed her chances of splitting the Chinese trio), to win her 1,500m heat and qualify for the final, her second-choice event. The Chinese factor dominated analysis prior to the final as awe and disbelief reverberated through the world of international athletics at the extent of the Chinese dominance of the women's middle-distance events in Stuttgart. The reigning world and Olympic champion Hassiba Boulmerka (Algeria) and the silver medallist from the Barcelona Olympics, Lyudmila Bogachova, qualified for the final along with three Chinese athletes including Liu Dong, the 1992 world junior champion. Liu Dong charged to the front from the start and deliberately slowed the pace, leading through an unspectacular 68.2-second first lap and an even slower second lap (69.4). The serious racing began at the 800m mark as Liu made a break accompanied by Lu Yi. Liu covered the third lap in 60.1 but Boulmerka, O'Sullivan and Lu were within a second of the leader. Liu continued to push the pace and a 57-second final 400m destroyed the chasers. In the race for silver, Lu and O'Sullivan passed Boulmerka on the curve and O'Sullivan raced into second place but was unable to reduce Dong's

25m advantage. Boulmerka recovered to take the bronze medal. In the words of O'Sullivan, 'All the tension that had been building up in the stadium throughout a week of suspicion and accusations suddenly exploded. The place went wild. Poor Liu Dong did her lap of honour to near silence in the stadium.' A medal presentation ceremony was staged prior to the start of the 1,500m final in Stuttgart and influenced O'Sullivan's tactical approach. In a post-final comment, she explained that she initially planned 'to run with any pace and then I changed my mind and decided to run for a medal'.

The greatest quantum leap in women's athletics history is now totally discredited. In February 2016 it was widely reported that a letter written in 1995 by Wang Juxia, the 3,000m world champion, and allegedly signed by nine of the most prominent athletes coached by Junren, had entered the public domain in China. Wang alleged that she and her team mates were forced to take 'large doses of illegal drugs over the years'. In the letter, she stated that women on the team tried to secretly throw away the pills forced on them. She also alleged that Ma Junren injected drugs into the athletes in his care. The IAAF, in its investigation of the matter, requested the Chinese Athletics Association for its support in establishing the validity of the letter. If the letter is confirmed as an admission of guilt by the athletes, they could be stripped of their titles and, as Sonia O'Sullivan finished in fourth place in Stuttgart in the 3,000m, she may eventually have two shiny gold World Championship medals added to her substantial portfolio.

BUDAPEST 1998: SONIA O'SULLIVAN, DUAL EUROPEAN CHAMPION

Sonia O'Sullivan shocked the athletics world in 1998 by winning both cross-country titles on offer at the World Championships in Marrakech, Morocco. Despite the victories, the comeback from the setback at Atlanta in 1996 wasn't complete and O'Sullivan struggled on the European track circuit over the summer months, where she competed mainly at 1,500m while her training regime, designed in association with her new coach Alan Storey, was geared towards the longer distances. She arrived in Budapest for the European

Championships with a 2–8 win–loss record, the two wins coming in Irish races.

The European Championships schedule facilitated athletes wishing to attempt a 10,000/5,000m double and the possibilities appealed to O'Sullivan, as she explained in *Sonia*. The longer distance 'had been taking up most of the space in my imagination for a while. I like new things. Ribeiro, the Olympic champion was going to be racing. I liked the challenge … I had nothing to lose. It was half an hour out of my life. No heats to run or anything.'

Sonia O'Sullivan made her debut at 10,000m in the European final with a simple tactic 'to keep up for as long as possible'. The slow first half of the race made the task easier; despite the leisurely pace the field had split into two groups after four laps with the likely winners in the lead group of O'Sullivan, Ribeiro, Julia Vaquero, Paula Radcliff and Lidia Simon. After 8,000m, Paula Radcliff surged without impact and then Ribeiro attempted a break. This too proved to be futile and at the bell the lead group of Ribeiro, Radcliff and O'Sullivan remained intact and Sonia O'Sullivan's winning debut at 10,000m was practically guaranteed. At 200m from the finish O'Sullivan lengthened her stride and drew away from Ribeiro 'like I was being carried on the wind', and with a time of 31:29.33 crossed the line 3 seconds ahead of her Portuguese rival. 'I'd made breaks like this hundreds of times in races but not one of them felt better than this,' she tells us in *Sonia*.

O'Sullivan's attention immediately turned to the 5,000m where she believed 'there was a medal there for the taking'. Gabriela Szabo was the main threat to the O'Sullivan double and, in the final, after an opening lap close to walking pace, Szabo took control of the pacemaking. O'Sullivan remained at her shoulder and studiously ignored her promptings to share in the pacemaking duties, much to the Romanian's chagrin. Szabo's most significant break 500m from the finish coincided with an O'Sullivan lapse in concentration as she drifted back to fourth place. It was a temporary lapse; O'Sullivan recovered and at the last bend she kicked to victory in a time of 15:06.50. For the first and only time in Irish athletics history, an athlete representing Ireland had achieved a double victory at a major athletics championships and *Amhrán na bhFiann* was played twice in 4 days, this time to recognise the achievements of a single athlete. The national anthem hasn't been played since to mark an Irish victory at the European Championships.

In the European Championships in Munich (2002), O'Sullivan finished in second place in both events. In the 10,000m she set an Irish record (30:47.59) to come second behind Paula Radcliffe; in the 5,000m 'a silly tactical error' cost her the gold medal; she was beaten by 0.09 seconds by Spanish distance runner Marta Domínguez. Since then, Derval O'Rourke performed brilliantly to win silver medals in the 100m hurdles in 2006 and 2010 while Mark Carroll (5,000m, 1998), Robert Heffernan (20km walk, 2010) and Mark English (800m, 2014) have won bronze medals. In 2010 Derval O'Rourke produced her season's best time to qualify for the final, then ripped over the hurdles in a new national record of 12.65 seconds, finishing second just 0.02 of a second behind Nevin Yanit (Turkey). Her 2006 silver medal was also accompanied by a national record of 12.72 seconds.

Ciara Mageean is the last Irish athlete to have won a European Championship medal. In 2016, the heir-apparent to Sonia O'Sullivan salvaged her career from long-term injury and won a bronze medal in the 1,500m. As a junior athlete, her performances surpassed those of both O'Sullivan and Szabo. In 2009, in Tampere at the European Youth Olympic Festival (EYOF), Mageean was a spectacular winner of the 1,500m title with a new EYOF record of 4:15.46, and in the process broke Gabriela Szabo's 1991 record and Sonia O'Sullivan's Irish junior record.

9

THE MAGIC OF THE MILE

ROGER BANNISTER BREAKS THE
PSYCHOLOGICAL BARRIER

The IAAF's history, *IAAF 1912–2012*, contains just a single chapter devoted to the history of an event. The mile, 'an anomaly in a metricated sport', is chosen as it 'retains a special and glorious place in the history of athletics'. Part of this glory connects to the event that took place on 6 May 1954 when Roger Bannister strode onto the Iffley Road track in Oxford, England, and emerged 3 minutes and 59.4 seconds later as the first athlete in history to run a mile in less than 4 minutes. Bannister broke a threshold many considered impossible in a carefully planned 'race' in which Barrister's friends Chris Brasher and Chris Chataway combined for the necessary and essential pace-making duties.

Sports Illustrated, in its very first issue of 16 August 1954, explained that the art of running the mile demanded that the athlete reach 'the threshold of unconsciousness at the instant of breasting the tape. It is not an easy process ... for the body rebels against such agonizing usage and must be disciplined by the spirit and the mind. Few events in sport offer so ultimate a test of human courage and human will and human ability to dare and endure for the simple sake of struggle – classically run, it is a heart-stirring, throat-tightening spectacle.'

IRELAND AND THE IRISH

Irish athletes have a distinguished record in the event and have broken every barrier associated with it: four of them have held the world 4 x 1 mile relay record since 1985, another has run 101 sub-4-minute miles, two have broken the sub-3:50 figure for the distance, one of whom was the first 40-year-old to run the distance in less than 4 minutes. A number have also established world records for the distance, particularly those who raced indoors in the USA.

A total of 326 sub-4-minute miles have been recorded in Ireland at ten different locations and fourteen different arenas. This includes Paul Robinson's 3:57.98 and Ben St Lawrence's 3:59.98 achieved at the Galway Regional Sports Centre as part of the Galway-Kenya Charity Run held on 14 September 2013. Their runs completed a missing link as this was the first occasion a sub-4 mile was recorded in Connacht. The magic figures have been reached in Dublin most often (149) at Santry Stadium and at the UCD track at Belfield; Cork is next with 120 achieved at the Mardyke and the Cork Institute of Technology venue; Belfast's 37 sub-4-minute miles have been recorded at Paisley Park, Aircraft Park and the Mary Peters Stadium. Leixlip, Tullamore, Tullylease, County Cork, Limerick and Letterkenny have each recorded three sub-4 miles. The most recent addition to the list of venues has been the Athlone Institute of Technology's indoor arena, where Ben Blankenship (USA) ran the first indoor sub-4-minute mile in Ireland (3:56.76) on 18 February 2015; since then the barrier has been broken on four more occasions in Athlone.

A total of forty-one Irish athletes have run sub-4 minutes, ranging from Ray Flynn's superb 3:49.77 of 7 July 1982 to Brian Treacy's 3:59.91 of 7 August 1999 achieved in London. The most recent Irish athlete to join the sub-4 club was Thomas Cotter (3:58.54), who achieved the distinction on 24 July 2015 in the Morton Mile. In addition, at least nine athletes from Northern Ireland who have competed mainly under the banner of Great Britain have broken 4 minutes for the distance. These athletes are Jim McGuinness, Derek Graham, Gary Lough, Steve Martin, Paul Lawther, Peter McGolgan, James McIlroy, Mark Kirk and Davey Wilson.

TOMMY CONNEFF: AN EARLY RECORD BREAKER

Tommy Conneff from Clane, County Kildare entered the world of athletics shortly after the foundation of the GAA. He first competed in local sports events in Kildare in 1885 and within a short time attained the status of a scratch athlete. As a member of Haddington Harriers he won the IAAA 880yd and 4-mile title in 1886 and the 1-mile title in 1887 in the new Irish record time of 20:55.8. In mid-January 1888, Conneff emigrated to the USA. On his departure, his colleagues in the William O'Brien GAA Club in Clane presented him with a wallet of sovereigns as well as an address which read, 'Dear Mr. Conneff, God speed you on your long journey and long may you live to bear the title of champion of the world'.

On his arrival in New York, Conneff announced that he 'never did any running at home excepting for my own amusement. Any exhibitions that I may enter here will be done for the same reason …'. Conneff returned briefly to Ireland as part of a joint NYAC and Manhattan AC team that visited Ireland and England in 1888. The party were welcomed to Kingstown where the:

> harbour was crowded with boats filled with athletes and their friends …, and a pleasure boat bearing a committee and a host of gentlemen interested in athletics waiting to escort them to Dublin … the appearance of the Americans was the signal for a prolonged cheering by the crowd ashore and afloat.

Conneff successfully defended his Irish title as a member of Manhattan AC on 21 May 1888 and on 30 June at Crewe won the AAA mile title. He also won both versions of the USA 1-mile title to complete an extraordinary quartet of titles for the distance in 1888.

Conneff was one of the leading middle-distance runners in the USA and won the USA 5-mile title 5 years in succession (1888–1891). On 21 August 1895, he set a world-best time of 3:02.8 for the ¾ mile despite working an overnight shift as a Pullman car conductor; this mark broke his own record of 3:07 set in Cambridge, Massachusetts on 26 August 1883. This record was established as Conneff set his first world-best mile mark (4:17.8). He drifted out of athletics after these records but he was persuaded to return for the international contest between London AC and New York AC staged in Manhattan on 21 September 1895. Like Mike Sweeney, Conneff engaged in a strict training programme designed by Mike Murphy of New York AC in the weeks before the contest. On 28 August, in a race designed to attack the existing world-best time, Tommy Conneff, paced by Eddie Carter for the last lap, ran the fastest mile of the nineteenth century at Travers Island, New York. His time of 4:15.6 was not surpassed until May 1911 and by an Irish athlete until 9 August 1947, when John Joe Barry set a new mark for an Irish athlete. Five days later, on 5 September, he established a new mark for the 2,000m when running 5:38.8 in Bayonne, New Jersey at the New Jersey Athletics Club Annual Labor Day Carnival. In the international contest, Conneff was an easy winner of the 1-mile and 3-mile events; Mike Sweeney in the high jump and James Mitchel in the hammer throw also contributed victories as the New York team won all eleven events. Conneff retired from athletics in 1895 and flirted for a while with the professional side of the sport. James Joyce included Conneff in *Ulysses* as one 'of many Irish heroes and heroines of antiquity'. He later joined the American Army on the outbreak of the American-Spanish War and while serving in the Philippines was drowned near Manila in October 1912.

JOHN JOE BARRY: THE BALLINCURRY HARE MAKES AN IMPRESSION

In *The Ballincurry Hare*, the biography of John Joe Barry, Noel Carroll described Barry as a man who 'led the life of a classical Irishman. A true character in terms of ability, outstanding achievement, colourful lifestyle and unfulfilled promise … He had the natural talent to achieve untold deeds on the running track, but somehow lacked the drive, the ambition and the dedication to see it through.' Appropriately, the colourful Barry enjoyed the rare privilege of living to read his own obituary, as, like Mark Twain in an earlier age, rumours of Barry's death were greatly exaggerated and 18 years premature when widely reported in 1976.

John Joe Barry was born in Joliet, Illinois, about 20 miles south of Chicago, on 5 October 1924 and returned to live in The Commons,

County Tipperary 3 years later. During the war years, Barry joined the Local Defence Force (LDF) where his natural talent for running was recognised. He subsequently joined the local Ballincurry AC and in 1945 enjoyed a summer of local success. He followed this by winning the county, provincial and national junior and senior cross-country championships in what was an extraordinary sweep of titles. Reservoirs of stamina developed working on the family farm combined with a latent natural running ability ensured that Barry quickly established a national profile. Barry made his Dublin track debut in 1945 at Croke Park and later in the year won the NACAI Irish Mile Championship at Dundalk and the 4-mile title at Ballinasloe and in 1946, the 880yd and 1-mile NACAI titles. He was recruited to the AAUE cause by Billy Morton and this switching of allegiance opened the door to international competition. As a member of Clonliffe Harriers he won the AAUE 880yd, 1- and 3-mile national titles in 1947. On 9 August 1947, he ran 4:15.2 and established a new Irish record for the mile.

Life in Dublin provided new social opportunities and distractions for Barry. He recalled in his biography *The Ballincurry Hare* that the move to Dublin transformed his social life:

I didn't drink or smoke, saved all my money, got a new suit, shirts, tie and shoes – and decided this was for me, I did all my training in The Teachers [Club], the National Ballroom and Barry's Hotel. In between I ate ice-cream in Caffola's in O'Connell Street … I went dancing in Parnell Square every night.

Hopelessly in love with a Scottish girl and attracted by the prospect of earning substantial under-the-table expense payments on offer in Scottish athletics, Barry moved to Glasgow in the winter of 1947, where he was employed as a clothes' salesman. A novice to international competition and clearly unfit, Barry failed miserably to make an impression at the 1948 Olympic Games. However, in 1949 Barry was a different athletic animal and over a period of 11 weeks, from 7 June to 27 August, he reduced the Irish miler record on three occasions from 4:14.0 to 4:08.6 – the latter on a grass track at College Park was particularly noteworthy. He also established new Irish records for the 2,000m, and the 2 and 3 miles (a brilliant 13:56.2 on the grass of Lansdowne Road). In 1949, he also won the Scottish

AAA and the AAA 3-mile titles. Back in Scotland at Helenvale Park, Glasgow, on Monday 13 June 1949, Barry scorched over 1½ miles in 6:33.8, a new world record for the distance, in what was his seventh major race in 9 days. When he won the 1950 American indoor-mile title he held simultaneously Irish, Scottish, English and American mile titles and accepted a scholarship to Villanova College in 1950.

The 1949 season was the high point in the career of a wonderful, naturally talented athlete; in his biography, he frankly admits that he fell into a cycle of drink, drugs and womanising in the USA, and outlines his own battles with alcoholism.

COMPTON 1956: RONNIE DELANY WASTES NO TIME

In late May 1956, Ronnie Delany and the Villanova College track team, unencumbered by examination pressures, ponied into Compton, California for the Compton Invitational meet. Delany and Gunnar Nielsen, the 1,500m world-record holder, were the stand-out runners in the Compton Mile held on 1 June 1956. Pacemaker Danny Schweikart set the early pace as Delany ran his typical race staying in the pack but maintaining contact with the leaders. Nielsen and two American runners, Fred Dwyer and Bobby Seaman, exchanged the lead several times over the first three laps. In Delany's words, 'The final lap was a scorcher', but as he explained in *Staying the Distance*, 'I had no idea how fast we were going or, more important, that we were on schedule for a four-minute mile'. In typical fashion, Delany edged in front 40yd from the finish and crossed the line marginally ahead of Nielsen. His time of 3:59 made Ronnie Delany the seventh and at the time the youngest member of the most exclusive club in the world of sport: the men who had run a mile in less than 4 minutes. Nielsen (3:59.1) also joined Bannister, John Landy, Laszlo Tábori, Chris Chataway, Brian Hewson and Jim Bailey in the ranks of the barrier breakers.

In *Staying the Distance*, Delany explained the significance of the achievement in a 'proper race'. They:

> ... ended a lot of drivel at that time about the psychological aspects
> of four-minute miling. There was no resolution here on either side,

no great tactical planning for our achievement. Rather two men pitted against each other had run as fast as they could in an effort to defeat the other and in the process had run four minutes.

MAGIC IN SANTRY STADIUM 1958: HERB ELLIOTT BREAKS THE 3:55 BARRIER

Herb Elliott was an athletic phenomenon. In his international career, which began in 1957 and ended in 1962, he was never beaten in forty-six races over the 1,500m/1 mile distance. He briefly retired from the sport in 1955 but a visit to the Melbourne Olympics restored his enthusiasm and he remained in Melbourne where he was coached by Percy Cerutty. A string of world junior best times confirmed the Elliott potential and in February 1958 he ran his first sub-4-minute mile.

One of the great nights in Elliott's career happened in Santry Stadium, Dublin on 6 August 1958. In typical flamboyant fashion, Billy Morton billed the race as the Golden Mile and he assembled a top-class field for the occasion, which included the Olympic 1,500m champion Ronnie Delany, the Australian world 3-mile record holder Albert Thomas, the Olympic 1,500m finalist Merv Lincoln as well as the 20-year-old Elliott. Over 20,000 spectators crushed into the Santry venue, officially opened in May 1958, on an evening that was ideal for middle-distance running.

The staging of the Empire Games in Cardiff in July 1958 provided an opportunity too great to be ignored by Billy Morton. Athletes arrived early in Cardiff and the flamboyant promoter persuaded several to travel to Dublin where he explained the Santry track was one of the world's fastest. The wily Morton also suggested that the trees surrounding the stadium pumped extra oxygen into the air, a process that added to the record-breaking potential of the venue. Some athletes travelled to Dublin for a meet on 7 July 1958 and when Albert Thomas set a new world-record time for the 3 miles (13:10.8), Morton's yarn spinning was given added credibility. This convinced some of the leading middle-distance runners to return to Dublin before going home from the Empire Games. The Australians and New Zealanders returned, as did some Canadian athletes.

In the Golden Mile, Albert Thomas took the runners through the first two laps in 1:58; Elliott took over at the beginning of the third lap and pushed the pace. He was chased by Merv Lincoln and, as Elliott explained in his biography *The Golden Mile*:

> On the bend, it was Lincoln not Delany who shot past me, I have never known him to do such a thing at this stage in a race before. I was thunderstruck. He must have been feeling as buoyant as me, I wouldn't have considered that possible ... Lincoln held the lead for 50 or 60 yards then as the bell sounded I nipped past him putting in a long burst. The time was 2:57. I was on my own now ... I drove my feet into those kind resilient cinders and flew.

And fly he did, crossing the line in 3:54.5, 2.7 seconds inside the existing world record. On one of the greatest nights in Irish athletics history, the first five athletes had run under 4 minutes for the first time in a single race and four had broken John Landy's existing mile record of 3:58 (Derek Ibbotson's time 3:57.2 had yet to be formally ratified). Mervyn Lincoln finished second (3:54.5), Ronnie Delany and Murray Halberg returned the same time (3:57.5) and Albert Thomas finished in fifth place (3:58.6). The following evening, Albert Thomas, paced by Herb Elliott, raced to a 2-mile world record (8:32) and Murray Halberg set a world-best time for the 4 miles (18:22); Santry Stadium for a brief spell was the centre of the athletics universe. This was the third and final time Delany broke the sub-4-minute barrier. His second was in London, in July 1957, when Derek Ibbotson established his new world mark and Delaney was runner-up (3:58.58). All three marks were new national records.

THE FIRST TEN

Ronnie Delany may have wasted no time in breaking the sub-4-minute barrier but over the next decade only two Irishmen achieved the feat. The first was Basil Clifford who ran 3:59.8 at the White City in London in the Emsley Carr Mile on 3 August 1964. Clifford was at the opposite end of the athletics spectrum to Delany; he worked in the Tony Farrell Bakery in Blackrock, County Dublin where part of his daily work routine involved carrying bags of flour up the steps of the shop on his back. The third to join the exclusive club was Derek Graham, a member of the Annadale Striders Club in Belfast. He was the first athlete from Northern Ireland to break the barrier when he ran 3:59:40 when finishing fifth at the Commonwealth Games in Kingston, Jamaica on 13 August 1966.

Athlete	Date	Venue	Time
Ronnie Delany	1 June 1956	Compton, USA	3:59
Basil Clifford	3 August 1964	White City, London	3:59.8
Derek Graham	13 August 1966	Kingston, Jamaica	3:59.4
Frank Murphy	1 June 1968	Philadelphia, USA	3:58.6
John Hartnett	12 May 1973	Eugene, Oregon	3:58.3
Eamonn Coghlan	10 May 1975	Pittsburgh, USA	3:56.2
Jim McGuinness	30 August 1975	Stretford	3:59.2
Niall O'Shaughnessy	1 May 1976	Fayetteville, North Carolina	3:58.1
Paul Lawther	19 June 1976	London	3:58.49
Gerry Kiernan	19 June 1976	London	3:59.12

A EUROPEAN RECORD AT KINGSTON, JAMAICA

An estimated 36,000 people massed into the National Stadium in Kingston, Jamaica on 17 May 1975 to witness the Drean Mile staged as part of the International Freedom Games, a nomadic track meet held in honour of Dr Martin Luther King and promoted by Bert Lancaster. Those present were privileged spectators to one of the great displays of front running in athletics history delivered by Filbert Bayi. At the end of the four laps, Bayi had shaved 0.1 seconds off Jim Ryun's 8-year-old world record of 3:51.1 and became the first African athlete to hold the world's mile record. Eamonn Coghlan was the one who chased the Tanzanian until the final furlong when he was overtaken by Marty Liquori who had supported Coghlan in chasing down Bayi. As they approached the bell, Coghlan was on Bayi's shoulder with Liquori who finished second in 3:52.2, the fifth-fastest mile in history at the time. Eamonn Coghlan's third-place finish in 3:53.3 set a new Irish and European record and ranked eleventh on the all-time list. Michael Jazy's record of 3:53.6 had survived for 20 years and was a world record when achieved in June 1965. Just a week earlier Coghlan had broken the 4-minute barrier for the first time in Pittsburgh (3:56.2) and had risen from the relative obscurity of an American college athlete to become an international star.

A WORLD RELAY RECORD IN BELFIELD, 17 AUGUST 1985

At the Weltklasse meet in Zurich in August 1985, John O'Shea, founder of GOAL, 'a third world relief organisation' that in 1985 had raised almost £2.5 million for the relief of suffering amongst the poor of the world, recruited three of the world's leading milers – Frank O'Mara, Marcus O'Sullivan and Ray Flynn – to form an Irish team with Eamon Coghlan and attempt a new world 4 x 1-mile relay record. Coghlan hesitated. He had missed the entire summer season with an assortment of injuries and most of his training had been confined to the swimming pool and the bicycle because of this. A week before the record attempt he had run 4:22 in a road race in Minneapolis where Ray Flynn witnessed his poor form.

The Longford athlete and his colleagues were not as keen as O'Shea to have Coghlan on board; however, he was important to the occasion for promotional and athletic reasons and the uncompromising O'Shea was in no mood to listen to any excuses. Coghlan was chosen to anchor the team and was pitted against John Treacy in the opening leg because, as Coghlan later recorded in *Chairman of the Boards*, 'they knew that pride alone would force me to stay ahead of John, especially over a mile'. In the meet billed as the GOAL National Sports Day and held at Belfield, Dublin on 17 August 1985, Treacy pushed Coghlan all the way and he handed over the baton to Marcus O'Sullivan after running the opening leg in 4:00.2; O'Sullivan's leg of 3:55.3 was the fastest of the four, Frank O'Mara was marginally slower in 3:55.6 before Ray Flynn brought the baton home in 3:56.98 for a cumulative time of 15:49.08, which smashed the existing record of 15:59.57 held by New Zealand. It hasn't been beaten since.

NORTHERN IRELAND'S FIRST: KIP KEINO BREAKS 4 MINUTES IN PAISLEY PARK

The Albert Foundry Football Club's modest Paisley Park base, on Belfast's West Circular Road, was the unlikely venue for the first sub-4-minute mile recorded in Northern Ireland. In the 1960s, the venue regularly hosted high-profile athletics meets and, on 16 August 1967, the great Kenyan athlete Kip Keino was a late addition to the field. On a wet and windy night, cheered by a crowd of over 2,000 spectators, he raced to victory in a time of 3:57.2. Keino was chased home by Derek Graham, who reported to Paisley Park after a day's work and became the first Northern Ireland athlete to break the 4-minute barrier in his own country with a time of 3:59.4. This was the second of three sub-4-minute miles Graham achieved during his career. Keino, Graham and Ian McCafferty (Scotland) reached the bell in 2:58 to make the barrier-bursting feat possible. Keino covered the last lap in under 60 seconds to complete the historic triumph. His time was almost 8 seconds faster than any previous recorded time for a mile in Northern Ireland.

THE FAMILY SUB-4

On 28 January 2012 at the Terrier Indoor Invitational meet at Boston University, John Coghlan finished third in 3:59.32 for his first sub-4-minute mile and joined his father Eamonn in the élite sub-4-milers club. Eamonn's first sub-4 mile of 3:56.2 was achieved in Pittsburgh on 10 May 1975. The Coghlans became the first Irish father–son combination to achieve the distinction and entered an even more rarefied group as only the seventh father–son combination to have done this. Since then, three more family combinations have joined the club. The first pair to break 4 minutes was two-time Olympic champion and running legend Kip Keino and his son Martin, who clocked 3:54.2 (1965) and 3:58.73 (1994) respectively. John Coghlan took time out from his studies at Dublin City University to compete in the US indoor circuit with the specific goal of breaking the 4-minute barrier. Victory on the night went to 23-year-old Providence College student David McCarthy, from Waterford, who also improved his previous mile best of 3:57.75 to a very impressive 3:55.75, a record for the Boston track.

RAY FLYNN'S DREAM MILE: 7 JULY 1982

Ray Flynn was the eleventh Irish middle-distance runner to record a sub-4-minute mile. In the 3-year period 1981–1983, Flynn ran under 4 minutes on forty-four occasions in what was an extraordinary strike rate, as he accumulated eighty-nine during his career. In the early 1980s, the Dream Mile was the stand-out event in Oslo and attracted the world's greatest milers to the storied arena. The star attraction at the 1982 event was Steve Scott, who cracked the 3:50 barrier there in 1981 when he established a new USA record of 3:49.68, topping Jim Ryun's 14-year-old mark; in 1982, 11 days before the Dream Mile, he again set the US mile record with a 3:48.53. On 7 July 1982, Scott, on a world record-breaking mission, joined a field that included the world's first sub-3:50 miler, John Walker, and Ray Flynn.

Mark Fricker took the field through the first two laps in 1:52.7 before dropping back midway through the third lap. Scott hit the front and was chased strongly by Ray Flynn but his finishing time of 3:47.69 was just short of Sebastian Coe's world record (3:47.33). In the final sprint for the line, Flynn was overtaken by Walker, whose time of 3:49.08 established a still-standing New Zealand national record. Ray Flynn's time of 3:49.77 was and remains the fastest time by an Irish athlete.

MARCUS O'SULLIVAN'S 101 SUB-4-MINUTE MILES

Marcus O'Sullivan is one of only three athletes to have broken the sub-4 barrier more than 100 times during his career. He joined John Walker (124 sub-4 miles) and Steve Scott (136) on 13 February 1998 when he finished in third place in the Wanamaker Mile at the Milrose Games at Madison Square Garden, New York in a time of 3:58.1. It was an appropriate occasion as O'Sullivan had won the famous indoor mile on five occasions. O'Sullivan, the last Irish athlete recruited to Villanova by the legendary coach Jumbo Elliott, ran his first sub-4-minute mile (3:58.84) on 22 January 1983 in the notoriously slow indoor arena in Chapel Hill, North Carolina. Finding his Chapel Hill trophy in the basement of his New Jersey home inspired O'Sullivan to chase the dream of a century of sub-4 miles. O'Sullivan explained on the historic occasion:

> I was thinking of retiring from athletics. I was cleaning out my basement when I came across the trophy I won for my first sub-4 in Chapel Hill in 1983 ... That's when I decided to go for the 100, which means entry to a pretty exclusive club ... It has helped greatly to keep me motivated over the past several seasons.

The quest had been immensely rewarding and life enhancing for the Leevale athlete:

> I've learned more about myself and the sport and training and what to do and what not to do than ever before in my life. It's like a light came on in a room and I knew for the first time where everything was. I don't believe I would have reached that pinnacle of understanding had it not been for the circumstances that have me here tonight.

Marcus O'Sullivan's final sub-4 mile (3:56.35) – his 101st – took place 12 days later in Melbourne, Australia on 25 February 1998. He also ran the metric equivalent of the sub-4 mile (i.e., sub 3:42.2 over 1,500m) an additional eighty-three times in a career of staggering consistency. The streak of 101 magnificent miles was achieved over a period of 15 years and 1 month.

THE FASTEST AND THE MOST ...

Sydney Maree arrived in Cork to compete in the Harp International Mile at the Cork City Sports on 7 July 1982 with a world-record run on his mind. Unfortunately rain in the hours before the race, blustery conditions and pacemaking that was slightly below par scuttled his chances. There was some consolation for Maree as he recorded the fastest mile ever in Ireland. His 3:49.44 has never been matched and shattered John Walker's previous best of 3:52 recorded in UCD's Belfield track in July 1977, another magical night for Dublin athletics when eight runners dipped under the 4 minutes for the distance. Ross Donoghue led the runners through the first two laps and when the pace in the second lap dropped to 59.2 seconds, Maree was forced to lead from the front.

What then transpired was the greatest mile race staged in Ireland. Maree was pushed to the end by Steve Cram, who also ran a sub-3:50 mile to finish in second place (3:49.44) and ahead of the great John Walker in third place in 3:50.03. Graham Williamson in fourth place set a new Scottish record (3:50.65), Ray Flynn finished in fifth place (3:51.64) and was followed home by Wilson Waigwa (3:52.43), Thomas Wessinghage (3:52.92), Jack Buckner (3:53.44 – an 8-second improvement on his personal best) and Paul Lawther from Belfast who crossed the line in 3:59 in ninth place.

This was the first occasion when nine athletes broke 4 minutes for the distance in Ireland, but on 8 July 1986 all eleven finishers in the Harp Lager Mile at the Cork City Sports were under the 4-minute mark. Steve Ovett was chased home by Marcus O'Sullivan who held off Sydney Maree in third place. O'Sullivan was accompanied by four more Irish athletes in the less-than-4-minutes journey. Tommy Moloney was fifth, Gerry O'Reilly sixth and David Taylor seventh; Eugene Curran in tenth place broke the barrier for the first time. Earl Jones (USA) was the eleventh man to finish the historic race (3:58.98). This sub-4 harvest was equalled on 22 July 2016 at the Morton Mile in Santry Stadium when eleven runners covered a spread of 3:55.57 and 3:58.57 between the winner, Johnny Gregorek (USA) and the eleventh-place finisher, Paul Robinson (Ireland), the only Irish athlete in the field.

The 11-under-4 benchmark was surpassed in the Morton Mile at Santry Stadium on12 July 2017 when twelve athletes, including Ireland's Seán Tobin (3:58.7), broke the 4-minute barrier. Robert Domanic was first home (3:54.73) ahead of Australian Morgan McDonald (3:55.71) with Peter Callanan the twelfth fastest in 3:58.86.

10

IRELAND UNDER COVER

RATHMINES WAS FIRST

Indoor athletics meets began in the mid-nineteenth century. The earliest known reference to an indoor meeting is an announcement in *Bell's Life* on 16 January 1859 of a 'grand entertainment of rustic fetes' at London's Lambeth Baths. In the USA, the first indoor meeting was staged at the Young Men's Gymnastics Club in Cincinnati in 1861. In 1863, the West London Rowing Club organised a more formal athletics promotion under gaslight in London's Ashburnham Hall that included 100, 220, 440 and 880yd events as well as the triple jump. Madison Square Garden was opened in 1879 and staged indoor track-and-field events from the beginning.

In Dublin, William Hely, a prominent Rathmines cycle dealer and a leading figure in the Harp Cycling Club, promoted the first indoor athletics meet held in Ireland at the Palace Rink in Rathmines. Athletics events and four cycling races were held on the eleven laps to the mile track on 3 January 1912. Irish athletes have been successful in indoor athletics since the 1890s. Mike Sweeney established two world high-jump indoor bests in 1893 and a third one in 1894 in Boston (6' 6⅜"). Martin Sheridan won the AAU indoor shot-put title in 1906 before Pat McDonald dominated the event by winning eleven titles between 1909 and 1921. John Joe Barry won the USA indoor-mile title in 1950, and initiated a trail that was followed by Ronnie Delany, Eamonn Coghlan, Marcus O'Sullivan, Frank O'Mara and Niall Bruton.

WORLD CHAMPIONSHIPS

The first World Championships were staged at the Hoosier Dome in Indianapolis on 6–8 March 1987 and attracted 402 athletes representing eighty-four countries. The championships were an unprecedented success for Ireland's four-man team. Marcus O'Sullivan (1,500m) and Frank O'Mara (3,000m) won world titles and Paul Donovan finished in second place to O'Mara. Prior to the championships, Frank O'Mara had run the world's fastest indoor mile at Brown University in Rhode Island on 31 January and, after opening laps of 70.21 and 70.18 seconds, the 3,000m effectively became a mile race. Donovan and O'Mara, graduates of the University of Arkansas and coached by John McDonnell, shared the pace-making over the first six laps in the final (2:55.43 at 1,000m); the serious race began when Mark Rowland stepped up the pace on the eighth lap. Rowland held the lead until two laps from home when he was overtaken by Doug Padilla and Frank O'Mara. The final 400m was covered in just 56 seconds; Padilla led at the bell when O'Mara challenged and took the lead on the back straight, sprinting to his first World Championship gold (8:03.32). Paul Donovan finished strongly and made up three places in the last 100m to win the silver medal in what was a unique event in Irish athletics history. The 1,500m final produced one of the great races of the championships as Jim Spivey took the finalists through the opening 800m in 2:01.70. José Abascal then took the initiative and pulled away from the field but was chased down by Marcus O'Sullivan in the final lap and the two track warriors sprinted side by side down the final straight. Abascal countered O'Sullivan's first move but the Leevale athlete was the stronger and finished 0.09 seconds ahead of his Spanish rival. Eamonn Coghlan was the centre of controversy after a dramatic fall in the sixth lap of the second heat when he became entangled with Dieter Baumann. The Chairman of the Boards lost almost 30m but recovered magnificently over the last two laps and raced into a qualifying position. With the hard work done, he made a serious tactical error and eased up as he approached the finishing line and was overtaken by Baumann and Dave Campbell. The world-record holder's time was not fast enough to qualify as a fastest loser. Irish team manager Ronnie Long lodged an appeal which was surprisingly upheld by track referee John Chaplin, but after objections from Spain, Italy and Holland an IAAF Jury of Appeals reversed Chaplin's decision.

MARCUS O'SULLIVAN: TRIPLE WORLD CHAMPION

Marcus O'Sullivan travelled to the 1991 World Championships in Budapest as both world champion and world-record holder (3:35.6) in the 1,500m. He easily qualified for the final where the pace was comfortable for an athlete with O'Sullivan's speed. Sydney Maree took the finalists through the opening lap in 53.82 and to the 800m stage in 1:56.75. At the bell, O'Sullivan zipped past Maree and with a final lap of 26.83 won his second world title in relative comfort in a championship-best time of 3:36.64, over 1 second ahead of Hauke Fuhlbrügge (3:37.80). In 1993, O'Sullivan just missed out on a third World Championship medal when he finished in fourth place as the new world-record holder, Noureddine Morceli (Algeria), added the world title to his collection. O'Sullivan was still a contender in 1995 when the championships were held in Toronto. He easily qualified for the final and the athletics gods smiled on the Cork athlete as a slow and tactical final unravelled. It was the ideal race for O'Sullivan and with a last lap sprint of 26.14 he collected his third gold medal, winning in a time of 3:45.00, the slowest by far of his three title-winning races. 'I thought three would be too much to ask,' said O'Sullivan of his third world indoor gold. 'It was like playing poker out there and I guess you could say I ended with a royal flush as it was slow and tactical.' The significance of O'Sullivan's victories should never be underestimated as Noureddine Morceli, Hicham El Guerrouj and Haile Gebrselassie, three of the all-time greats over the distance, won the other four titles of the seven on offer between 1987 and 1999.

FRANK O'MARA: DUAL WORLD CHAMPION

In winning his second 3,000m title in Seville in 1991 Frank O'Mara produced one of the finest performances of his career. The event was top-heavy with quality and the qualifying heats produced six national records. There were six more records set in the final thanks to the early pace set by Jacinto Navarrete and Rob de Brouwer. Hammou Boutayeb took over at 2,000m (5:13.48) and only Frank O'Mara managed to keep pace with the veteran Moroccan. He went to the front; with two laps remaining he raced clear after 50m and won so easily that he allowed himself to celebrate on the final bend. O'Mara's winning time (7:41.14) was the fourth fastest in history and a new championship record.

DERVAL O'ROURKE: 60M HURDLES CHAMPION, 2006

Derval O'Rourke had never qualified for a final of a major championship prior to the 2006 World Indoor Championships in Moscow. After a winter devoted to strength, conditioning and technical work in association with her coaches Jim Kilty and Sean Cahill, as well as Dr Liam Hennessy, Dave Fagan and nutritionist Andrea Cullen, the omens were good prior to Moscow. At the Odyssey Arena in Belfast, she skimmed over the hurdles in 7.9 seconds to win the national 60m indoor title and improved her national record of 7.98 set in winning the British title a week earlier, when she became the first Irish athlete to break 8 seconds for the event. Earlier in the season, O'Rourke equalled her own national record (8.02). Derval confirmed her athletic and competitive well-being in Moscow and comfortably qualified for the semi-final with a second-place finish in the opening heat (7.93). A brilliant semi-final victory in another new national record (7.87) signalled the arrival of a potential new world champion.

In the final, Derval O'Rourke flew from the blocks and was never headed; she became the first Irishwoman to win a sprint title at a major championship and the only Irishwoman to win a world indoor title. She set another new national record (7.84) and edged Glory Olonzo out of the gold medal position by 0.02 seconds, also winning the €40,000 first-place prize money on offer. The victory began a new phase in O'Rourke's career and she established new national records in four of the five major international championships in which Irish athletes compete. A silver medal in the 100m hurdles at the European Athletics Championships at Gothenburg in August, with a sensational new Irish record of 12.72 seconds (her fourth of the season), confirmed O'Rourke's status as a brilliant world-class athlete and superb competitor with steel in her soul when others might be stressed. Sean Cahill's role in transforming Cahill into a major championship-winning hurdler was pivotal. In her *Irish Examiner* column, in which she announced her retirement, O'Rourke identified Sean and Terri Cahill as the coaches that 'basically turned my dreams and ambitions into reality. It seems unfair to have my name alone alongside the medals and records when they were such a massive part of every single one. Their coaching and high performance expertise has been phenomenal ... they are truly the best out there.'

SONIA TAKES SILVER ... IN PARIS 1997

Indoor running was never a high priority in Sonia O'Sullivan's bucket list. As she explains in *Sonia*, 'I have a long stride which isn't suited to indoor running generally ... some people just aren't meant to run indoors. I am one of those people.' However, in 1997, 'still just an athlete crawling out of the [Atlanta] wreckage', she flew directly from her Melbourne base to Paris to 'have a cut' at the 3,000m straight final in the World Indoor Championships and another showdown with Gabriela Szabo and Fernanda Ribeiro. It was O'Sullivan's first indoor race in 5 years. The Portuguese pair Marina Bastos and Ribeiro set the pace and were shadowed by O'Sullivan as Szabo lurked with intent behind the three front runners. On the penultimate lap, O'Sullivan broke clear. 'It felt great,' O'Sullivan explained in *Sonia*, 'except that Szabo came too, following intently as a secret policeman.' The Romanian maintained her position until the final bend when O'Sullivan moved out from the kerb and presented Szabo with a gap which the Romanian duly accepted and sprinted away to win the world title. Szabo's winning time was 8:45.75 with O'Sullivan just 0.44 seconds slower. Sonia returned to Australia with a World Championship silver medal and a clear explanation as to why it wasn't gold: 'Tactics. Tactics. Tactics.'

PAUL MCKEE: A SURPRISE BRONZE IN BIRMINGHAM, 2003

An Irish sprinter on the medallists' podium at a major athletics championship is a rare occurrence. Paul McKee is an exception to the rule that Irish sprinters do not win medals on such occasions and was a bronze-medal winner at the 2003 World Championships held in Birmingham. Unfortunately, McKee was denied the opportunity of standing on the podium for the medal presentation ceremony. Tyree Washington and Daniel Caines conducted their own private duel through the competition and finished first and second; the 1999 champion Jamie Baulch and semi-final winner Paul McKee (46.24) crossed the line together and were awarded a joint third place (45.99). This was later reviewed and Baulch was promoted to third place with McKee relegated to fourth place. The medal presentation ceremony took place without McKee, whose semi-final and final times were national records. However, a protest from Ireland was upheld and McKee was restored to a shared third position and received his bronze medal in a separate ceremony at the conclusion of the championships.

BUDAPEST 2004: AN UNLIKELY RELAY BRONZE

Irish relay quartets have produced some outstanding performances in major events, but the 4 x 400m men's relay team at the World Championships at Budapest are the only ones to medal. The quartet were the main beneficiaries of the disqualification of the USA for the third successive time in the world final. On the final changeover, Joe Mendel fell in the process of handing over to Godfrey Herring. The baton went free and was retrieved by the anchor man Herring who managed to retain third place despite the scramble for the baton behind winners Jamaica with Russia in second place. The USA were subsequently disqualified as the runner who drops the baton (Mendel) must retrieve it before the change. As a result, Ireland (Robert Daly, Gary Ryan, David Gillick and David McCarthy) was promoted to third place.

EUROPEAN CHAMPIONS

The European Indoor Athletics Championships were first staged in 1970; prior to this the European Indoor Games were held annually from 1966. Fittingly, Maeve Kyle was a bronze medallist at the inaugural games in the 400m; the 800m became the personal fiefdom of Noel Carroll who won the first four titles in the event. At the European Championships, four athletes have earned champion status: Eamonn Coghlan in the 1,500m (1979); Mark Carroll in the 3,000m (2000); double champion David Gillick in the 400m (2005 and 2007) and Alistair Cragg in the 3,000 (2005). The poster boys of Irish middle-distance running, Frank Murphy, Ray Flynn, Marcus O'Sullivan and Mark English, have won silver medals.

HOW TO BEAT DELANY – OOPS!

This was a headline used by *Sports Illustrated* to describe how Ronnie Delany 'sailed undefeated through one indoor race after another, through his rivals never stopping' as he assembled one of the finest winning streaks in the sport's history. The sequence began in Madison Square Garden on 25 March 1955 with a victory in the 1,000yd event at the New York Knights of Columbus meet and ended in Chicago on 28 March 1959 when Delany won the mile event at the *Chicago Daily News* meet in a time of 4:06.4. This was Delany's fortieth successive indoor victory and the last occasion he raced indoors in an individual race. A serious Achilles tendon injury shortly afterwards marked the beginning of the end of Delany's spectacular career. He was not to race again until the morning of 31 August 1960 in the Rome Olympics 800m heats. The unbeaten streak included thirty-four successive mile victories and such feats of athletic wonder as winning the 1,000yd and 2-mile events at the ICAAAA Intercollegiate Championships in 1957 and 1958 within a short time of each other, as well as establishing three indoor world bests. If victories in heats are included, the undefeated sequence stretches to forty-three races in what was truly an extraordinary feat of athletic excellence. Delany was only beaten twice indoors, once over 880yd and once over 1,000yd on 5 February and 19 February 1955 in what were the third and fifth indoor races of his career.

SEVEN WORLD RECORDS

Irish athletes have broken the world indoor mile or 1,500m record on seven occasions. The IAAF has officially ratified world indoor records since 1 January 1987 with the existing world indoor bests accepted as the inaugural world records. Ronnie Delany's three times belong to this 'world-best' era. Delany established his first world mark in Chicago on 14 March 1958 at the *Chicago Daily News* meet with a time of 4:03.4; almost a year later, at Madison Square Gardens, on 21 February 1959, he reduced the record to 4:02.5. On 7 March, at the same venue, he completed his trio of world-best marks when he recorded 4:01.4 in what was his last individual race in the famed venue. Delany's world-record treble was matched by Eamonn Coghlan who returned to the USA on a permanent basis after the Moscow Olympic Games and spent the winter months of 1981 in San Diego, where he set his first mile world best on 16 February 1979 (3:52.6). The Jack-in-the-Box Invitational meet on 20 February 1981 attracted two of the greatest milers in history, John Walker and Steve Scott, to San Diego to challenge Coghlan who had ambitions of breaking 3:50 in what was something of a grudge race with Scott. Coghlan recruited his former Villanova teammate Tiny Kane to do the pacemaking over the first 880yd. Kane fulfilled his side of the mission and took the athletes through to the halfway stage in 1:55.6. Steve Scott took over and with two laps to go Eamonn Coghlan made the decisive mover of the race and zipped through the finishing line in 3:50.6 – a new world best, the sixth fastest mile in history and the fastest recorded in America, but agonisingly Coghlan had narrowly missed out on his primary mission of doing a sub-3:50 run. On 10 February 1989, Marcus O'Sullivan set a new world 1,500m record of 3:35.6 on his way to winning the Vitalis Olympic Invitational Mile (3:51.66). Justice was done for O'Sullivan on this occasion as, at the same meeting in 1988, he won the mile in 3:50.94 and was timed at 3:35.4 in what would have been a new world best for 1,500m. Unfortunately, of the four watches in operation only one was stopped as the other timers were distracted by the excitement of the race.

THE FIRST SUB-3:50 INDOORS

In 1982, Eamonn Coghlan, the owner of fifteen of the twenty fastest indoor miles in the history of the sport at the time, was voted by track statisticians and writers as the greatest indoor miler in history. The injured Chairman of the Boards was 22 months without an indoor race when the award was made. A discussion with Thomas

Wessinghage at the Cork City Sports in July 1982 established a link with a German specialist who identified a tearing away of a tendon from the heel bone as the problem and months of frustration in search of a cure were ended. Coghlan made a successful comeback to the American scene in 1983 but 3 days after winning the Wanamaker Mile he awoke in his Rye home in upstate New York to discover that his father Bill had died overnight in his sleep. Coghlan returned to Dublin for his father's funeral and was a three-times winner on his return to New York, beating Ray Flynn twice and Steve Scott three times. The two most influential coaches in his career, Gerry Farnan and Jumbo Elliott, had also died in the previous year. On 27 February 1983, Eamonn Coghlan reported to the Brendan Byrne Arena in Meadowlands, New Jersey for the Vitalis/Olympic Invitation race with a sub-3:50 mile on his mind. The seven-man field included Steve Scott, José Abascal and Ray Flynn, three of the era's top milers.

Pacemaker Ross Donoghue took the field through the first 880yd in 1:55.7 and stepped off the track a little earlier than intended. Coghlan became the front runner and soon had the crowd of 11,741 on their feet as he reached the ¾-mile point in 2:54.8 – slightly outside his desired split but a second inside the 1981 San Diego world-record pace. With two laps remaining, Coghlan sprinted for glory. Ray Flynn moved past Steve Scott into second place but made no impression on Coghlan who similarly drew away from Flynn as he extended his lead to 8, 10 and finally 12yd. Coghlan crossed the line in a new world indoor-record time of 3:49.78. It was the first sub-3:50.0 indoor mile in athletics history and the first sub-3:50 mile achieved on American soil. Flynn finished in second place in 3:51.20, the third fastest indoor mile at the time and currently the ninth fastest ever recorded. Eamonn Coghlan's time has only been surpassed indoors once in the sport's history. On 12 February 1997, Hicham El Guerrouj (Morocco) set the current world record of 3:48.45 at Ghent in Belgium.

THE WANAMAKER MILE: AN IRISH SPECIALITY

The Millrose Games remains the outstanding indoor meet in the USA with the Wanamaker Mile, named after the department store founder Rodman Wanamaker, the signature event of the meet. Rodman resided in a Pennsylvanian estate known as Millrose. The event was first held in 1926 at New York's Madison Square Garden which hosted the event until 2012, when it was moved to the Armory in Upper Manhattan. The games are staged in February and the world's greatest milers have put their reputation on the line in the famous mile race which has produced forty-nine different champions since its inception; five of these have been from Ireland and between them they have won the race on nineteen occasions. Only milers from the USA have been more successful. Ronnie Delany began the trend with four successive wins (1956–1959); Eamonn Coghlan was next to step on the winner's podium in 1977 with the first of what proved to be a record-breaking seven wins. He also won three successive titles in 1979–1981 as well as in 1983, 1985 and 1987. Marcus O'Sullivan won six titles starting in 1986, three times from 1988 to 1990, and again in 1992 and 1996; Niall Bruton (1994) and Mark Carroll (2000) won a single title each.

The standing of the Wanamaker Mile and Coghlan's status in American athletics history are evident from Stuart Miller's 2006 book entitled *The 100 Greatest Days in New York Sports*. The night of 30 January 1987 is chosen as the ninetieth greatest day in the city's sports history. On this date, Eamonn Coghlan won his seventh Wanamaker title and surpassed Glen Cunningham's previous record of six titles. Marcus O'Sullivan was his main challenger and with a lap and a half remaining O'Sullivan made his key move. He led at the bell but Coghlan responded and in Miller's version of the race:

> The younger runner lacked Coghlan's grit and determination. Both seemed to know that too. With about 80 yards left, Coghlan zoomed outside and flew past Abascal and O'Sullivan. He won going away, five yards ahead, both fists raised in triumph. His time was 3:55.91, but most impressive was his final quarter-mile of 55.4 seconds.

Although beaten, O'Sullivan appreciated Coghlan's achievement. 'I had given everything I had and I was just so happy for him. It's good to see the old fellow back again,' he told the New York newsmen on the historic night.

Although the Irish high-profile presence at the Millrose Games belongs to a different era, one miler who did not win the feature event, Ray Flynn, has been the meet director for the past 6 years.

UNDER-4: OVER 40

Just as Roger Bannister was involved in a race against time in 1954, 40 years later Eamonn Coghlan was similarly engaged with John Walker, Rod Dixon and Dave Moorcroft in the chase to be the first athlete over 40 to record a sub-4-minute mile. Walker got injured, Dixon got sick and Moorcroft abandoned the quest. The chase ended on 20 February 1994 before 3,200 ecstatic spectators on the Albert J. Gordon Indoor Track at Harvard in Cambridge, Massachusetts in a special race included in the Massachusetts State High School meet.

Eamonn Coghlan retired in 1990 but returned in 1991 and prepared for the *Runner's World* Masters Mile, a series of races for the top male runners aged 40 and over. Coghlan became a masters runner in November 1992 and appropriately ran his first masters mile at the Millrose Games, where he had earned his reputation as the 'chairman of the boards'. In 1993, he established a world masters record of 4:01.39 on the Madison Square Garden's slow eleven laps to the mile track. The 1994 indoor season was Coghlan's last-chance-saloon opportunity to break the barrier and he moved to Gainesville, Florida in December 1993 where he worked daily with physical therapist Gerard Hartmann. Coghlan's Florida regime of 'training twice a day, distance running, track works, weights, stretching, ice packs ... Ger continuing to work away on the injuries two hours a day, six days a week' began to pay off, but he could do no better than 4:04.5 in winning the Masters Mile at the Millrose Games. However, 2 days later at Washington he ran 4:03.23 to raise his spirits. Unfortunately, enthusiasm for masters miles dwindled and the event was dropped from the US Indoor Championships scheduled for Atlanta. Al Franken in Los Angeles also dismissed the notion of staging a masters mile. On the advice of Victor Sailer, a New York firefighter, track fanatic and part-time photographer, Coghlan decided to travel to Cambridge for his final masters examination. Much of the race logistics were organised by Coghlan himself.

On the fast 200m banked synthetic oval track, paced by Stanley Redwine, Coghlan reached the ½-mile mark in 1:59.44 and the ¾-mile stage in 2:59.22. A sprinted last quarter of 58.93 created history and Coghlan crossed the line in a time of 3:58.15, to set a new world masters record. In *Chairman of the Boards, Master of the Mile*, Coghlan paints a vivid picture of the final stages of the race:

> With 150 yards to go my legs were buckling, they were all over the place, totally out of control, but the noise of the crowd told me I was on schedule. It was almost an out-of-body experience. The din increased to such a crescendo that I was able to momentarily forget the struggle my legs were undergoing. It was as if they belonged to somebody else. My ears literally hurt from the noise.

The 3:58.15 justified the pain:

> It was the most profound running experience of my life – different to anything that had gone before ... But to me it was an emotional and physical triumph beyond my wildest expectations. Nothing compared to the feeling of ecstasy that enveloped me when I crossed that line ... It was the most euphoric feeling I ever had in my life. All the pain, all the sacrifices and more importantly all my self-beliefs were tested beyond human endurance.

After running seventy-five sub-4-minute miles, 'the race was over, the puzzle complete. For the first time in years I could sleep peacefully, totally fulfilled', Coghlan explained in *Chairman of the Boards*. *Track and Field News* recognised the achievement by putting 'ageless Eamonn' on the cover and described how history was created under the headline 'The Old Man Does It'.

11

WOMEN AND IRISH ATHLETICS

SOPHIE PEIRCE-EVANS: EVANGELIST AND PRACTITIONER OF WOMEN'S ATHLETICS

One of the great early pioneers of women's athletics was Sophie Peirce-Evans who was born in Knockaderry, County Limerick on 10 November 1896. Within 13 months of her birth, Sophie was effectively orphaned as her mother Catherine was murdered by her husband Jackie, who was found guilty of the crime, but insane, and committed to the Criminal Lunatic Asylum in Dublin, where he remained until his death in 1916. Sophie was reared in nearby Newcastle West by her grandfather Dr George Peirce-Evans and her two aunts, Cis and Lou.

As a boarder in St Margaret's Hall School in Dublin, Sophie prospered academically and discovered sport, especially hockey and tennis. In 1914, she enrolled in the Royal College of Science in Ireland where she specialised in agricultural studies. While still a student, she married Captain William Eliott-Lynn, commanding officer of the Royal Irish Rifles, a man twice her age. Six months later she volunteered her services to the War Office and served as a motorcycle dispatch rider with the Women's Auxiliary Army Corps in France. She resumed her studies after the war and graduated in July 1921. In the meantime her husband had emigrated to east Africa and Sophie moved to London in March 1922 after a short spell in the University of Aberdeen.

Prior to emigrating, Sophie Eliott-Lynne added athletics to her sporting repertoire and competed in events in Dublin and elsewhere.

She was a winner in the high jump at the Dublin Tramway Sports in Lansdowne Road (4' 0"/1.22m) and at the Clonliffe Harriers Sports (4' 6"/1.37m). Her winning effort at the Tramway event was 'not a bad effort for the sex in these days of general male mediocrity', *Sport* noted.

Life in London provided new opportunities for Sophie to compete in athletics. In October 1921, the *Fédération Sportive Féminine International* (FSFI) was formed to provide an institutional framework and structure for promoting and managing women's sport. A year later, the Women's Amateur Athletics Association (WAAA) was formed with Sophie Eliott-Lynne a member of its first officer board. In August 1922, the FSFI organised the first Women's Olympic Games in Paris; Sophie was both a competitor and official for the WAAA team. She instructed the selected athletes to 'please provide yourself with close-fitting black knickers reaching to not more than 4 inches from the ground when kneeling, a loose white tunic of stout material belted, with elbow sleeves, reaching 10–12 inches below the waist ...', and finished in ninth place in the two-handed shot. After a winter spent in Africa with her husband, Sophie returned to London and resumed her athletics career. In the Monte Carlo Games, she finished in third place in both the high jump and javelin. In August 1923, the inaugural WAAA Championships were held and Sophie Eliott-Lynne won the javelin title, finished runner-up in the 120yd hurdles and was third in the shot-put. In September, she represented the Great Britain team in the annual international with France. Two of the high-jump marks from this phase of her career are listed in the IAAF progression book of world records: on 2 August 1922 at Torquay she cleared 1.47m (4' 10") and on 6 August 1923, at Brentwood, she cleared 1.485m (4' 10½"). After again wintering in Africa, Sophie joined the Middlesex Ladies Athletics Club and became an advocate of women's participation in sport as a means of promoting health: 'the heart which beats quickly, when its owner runs and chases the elusive ball, is the best of beauty doctors', she wrote. In 1924, Sophie recorded a double at the WAAA Championships, winning the high jump (1.45m) and the two-handed javelin with a superb 52.78m, the highlight of her competitive career and of her 1924 season.

At this stage women's athletics had yet to be included in the Olympic programme. In 1924, the IAAF decided to accept women's track and field but not to advocate its inclusion in the Olympic programme. The FSFI continued to agitate and, in 1925, Eliott-Lynne was a member of the FSFI delegation that attended a two-part IOC Session in Prague where she presented two papers to the pedagogical session. In a lecture entitled 'Women's Participation in Sport', she informed the august assembly that running was an ideal sport for women as were the field events: 'The swaying and bending movements entailed especially by the throwing events are invaluable from the point of view of improvement of intestinal circulation.' Her instructional manual *Athletics for Women and Girls: How to be an Athlete and Why* (1925), one of the first instructional manuals written for women by a woman, was published after she returned from Prague; the inclusion of a preface written by IOC member Brigadier Reginald Kentish, one of Britain's most eminent Olympic officials, was significant. The profits from its sale went to the WAAA and the Playing Fields Association. She was part of a British athletics team that toured Sweden in September 1925.

In 1926, the IOC bowed to the inevitable and accepted a restricted number of athletics events limited to the 100m, 800m, 4 x 100m relay, high jump and discus throw. The WAAA were so enraged at the limitation that they decided to boycott the 1928 Games. Eliott-Lynne was scheduled to officiate at Amsterdam as a member of the FESI but her name was withdrawn from the list when the British opted not to compete. Her association with athletics was marginalised after her return from Prague. Flying became her new passion and before the year ended she secured her solo pilot's licence and set numerous aeronautical records in her new obsession. She completed the first solo flight by a woman from South Africa to England (February–May 1928), stepped from her aeroplane in Croydon and announced that it was 'so safe that a woman can fly across Africa wearing a Parisian frock and keeping her nose powered all the way'.

JOHN CHARLES MCQUAID HAS HIS SAY: 'MIXED ATHLETICS ARE A SOCIAL ABUSE'

If the IOC and the IAAF accepted the inevitable, the NACAI was made of sterner chauvinistic stuff. Although the NACAI included a national 100yd championship for women in its programme from 1929 until 1933 (Maura Barrett (three) and Joan Baird (one) won the titles), women's athletics was effectively banned since the early 1930s in twenty-six-county Ireland. At the IAAF Congress of 1928, the Irish delegates voted against the proposal to introduce a comprehensive programme of women's athletics to the Olympic Games but unsuccessfully supported the introduction of the 800m, long jump, and 200m. In 1934, the annual congress of the NACAI approved a Dublin motion requesting 'that championships for women in Ireland be held in a limited number of events and that one event for women be inserted in each of the open meetings throughout the country'. The suggestion provoked an immediate negative response, with the president of Blackrock College, Rev. John Charles McQuaid, leading the charge. In a letter to the *Irish Times* (9 February 1934), McQuaid castigated the decision as 'un-Catholic and un-Irish' and concluded with the promise 'that no boy from my college will take part in any athletics meeting controlled by your organisation at which women will compete no matter what attire they may adopt'. McQuaid's intervention attracted widespread support. Encouraged by the response, he returned to the *Irish Times* on 24 February 1934 and pointed out that much that had been written since his original letter was 'painfully irrelevant'.

The issue was not about 'what forms of athletic sport may women or girls indulge with safety to their well-being'; neither was it a question of 'what form of athletic sport may girls or women indulge within the reserved territory of their own colleges and associations. Mixed athletics and all cognate immodesties are abuses that rightminded people reprobate, wherever, and whenever they exist.' In McQuaid's world view, modernity and mixed athletics were not mutually inclusive. 'It is a Christian duty, incumbent on us all,' McQuaid pointed out, 'not to adopt what is morally wrong. God is not modern; nor His Law.' McQuaid elaborated on his un-Irish and un-Catholic themes. The decision was un-Irish as mixed athletics were 'a social abuse' that outraged 'our rightful, national tradition', a claim that required 'only some reflection'. The decision was 'un-Catholic' as mixed athletics were 'a moral abuse'. McQuaid quoted verbatim from the encyclical *Divini Illius Magistri* of Pope Pius XI to support this claim. He helpfully provided a translation that in part advised that 'in athletic sports and exercises, wherein the Christian modesty of girls must be, in a special way, safeguarded; for it is supremely unbecoming that they should flaunt themselves and display themselves before the eyes of all'. McQuaid was well supported. Irish society at the time was male-dominated and deeply conservative. Faced with the challenge of papal teaching and clerical opposition, the NACAI's scheme to promote women's athletics was abandoned in March 1934 by a unanimous decision of the organisation's Central Council.

CRUSADERS ATHLETICS CLUB TRY AGAIN

The conservatism did not disappear at the end of the 1930s. John Charles McQuaid, appointed Archbishop of Dublin by Pope Pius XII in 1940, helped to slap down the next attempt to promote women's athletics in Dublin. In 1947, Crusaders Athletics Club established a women's section and by the end of 1949 thirteen senior and seven junior women were members. In 1947 two women's events were included in one of the Lansdowne Road programmes. Maeve Kyle won the high jump and her Pembroke Wanderers hockey colleague the 100yd. Kyle was part of the Crusaders innovation and trained for the summer of 1948 with the club's coach Joe O'Keeffe before travelling to Belfast to compete in the RUC Coronation Sports at Ravenhill, where she won the 80yd and 220yd events. Once again John Charles McQuaid intervened and, in a Lenten pastoral, young women competing in mixed cycling and athletic sports were subjected to McQuaid's 'grave disapproval' and included in an eclectic list that included atheistic communism, mixed marriages and pony racing on Sundays. The Crusaders initiative struggled and was abandoned in 1951 after concluding that 'the experience of its working unsatisfactory and believing that it has no real prospects'. The NACAI revisited the issue in 1957 and a Dublin motion calling on the association to actively promote women's athletics was passed 'with reservations' and promptly forgotten.

FANNY BLANKERS-KOEN COMES TO DUBLIN

The star of the 1948 London Olympic Games was Francine 'Fanny' Blankers-Koen (Netherlands), a veteran of the 1936 Berlin Games. Since 1936, she had married her coach Jan Koen and given birth to two children. At the 1948 Games she won gold medals in the 100m, the 80m hurdles, the 200m and the 4 x 100m relay. At this time, Billy Morton, a Dublin optician and secretary of the Clonliffe

Harriers Club, had established his legend as an extraordinary talented promoter of athletics meets. Thanks to Morton's genius at persuading leading international athletes to compete in Dublin, on 26 August 1948 Fanny Blankers-Koen competed in the Clonliffe Harriers Sports staged at Lansdowne Road. Morton had to advertise in the newspapers for sportswomen to compete against the Olympic champion. The meet coincided with Dublin Horse Show week and an estimated 25,000 crowded into the venue to see Blankers-Koen and her Dutch teammates. The great champion did not disappoint. She easily defeated British Olympian Audrey Williamson in her 100yd heat and in the final finished 5yd ahead of Dorothy Manley, the London 100m silver medallist, in a time of 10.8 seconds which equalled her own world-record time. Irish hockey international Joan O'Reilly of Crusaders AC finished in third place. She also won the 200yd by a distance from Audrey Williamson. Paul McWeeney of the *Irish Times*, like his reporter colleagues, was impressed and wrote that she was 'a delight to watch ... She has the long, controlled stride of the first-class male runner, yet she is more graceful than any man I have seen on the track'. Blankers-Koen returned to Dublin in 1949 and won the 100yd (11.2) and the 80yd hurdles (11.6).

NORTHERN IRELAND WAS DIFFERENT

In 1947 Queen's University Belfast established the first women's athletics club in Ireland. The university included women's events in its championship programmes in 1947; a women's athletics club was founded in the college the same year and competed in a triangular meet with St Andrew's and Glasgow University. Short and Harland AC was formed in 1948 after the visit of the Jamaican Olympic team to Belfast and in 1949 the NIAAA included four women's events in its championship programme. The Northern Ireland Women's Amateur Athletics Association (NIWAA) was formed in 1951 and the first women's championships were held the same year. The famous Austrian coach Franz Stampfl was hired to coach and promote women's athletics in Northern Ireland. Three outstanding women athletes emerged from Northern Ireland during the 1950s and represented their respective countries eight times at the Olympic Games.

THELMA HOPKINS: OLYMPIC MEDALLIST AND WORLD-RECORD HOLDER

Thelma Hopkins made her Olympic debut in Helsinki in 1952 as a 16-year-old representing Great Britain and finished in fourth place in the high jump. In Melbourne in 1956 she won a silver medal in the same event (1.67m). Hopkins was born in Hull on 16 March 1936 but the family moved to Belfast shortly afterwards. Hopkins was coached by Frank Stampfl and was a double gold medallist in 1954 at the British Empire and Commonwealth Games at Vancouver (1.67m) and at the European Championships in Berne (1.67m).

She secured a place in athletics history in Belfast on 5 May 1956 at Cherryvale Park, when she jumped 1.74m (5' 8½") to break the high-jump world record in a match between the NIWAAA, Queen's University and Manchester University. She was unable to reproduce this form in Melbourne where Mildred McDonald (USA) took the gold medal and set a new world record in the process (1.76m). Hopkins travelled to Australia three months before the Games to train with Stampfl, a plan that did not work as she had hoped, for she found it difficult to acclimatise and suffered from homesickness.

Hopkins was a superb all-round athlete who won WAAA titles in the high jump (1955, 1957), the long jump (1955) and 80m hurdles (1957) and won over thirty NIAAA titles. She represented Great Britain and Northern Ireland on twenty-six occasions in international competition and in August 1963 was a member of the first combined Ireland team that competed against Belgium in Santry Stadium. She also represented Ireland against Scotland in August 1964. She represented Northern Ireland at the Empire (Commonwealth) Games in 1954, 1958 and 1962. Like Maeve Kyle, Hopkins combined an international hockey career with her athletics career and earned forty-one international caps for Ireland between 1953 and 1965. She was inducted into the Irish Hockey Hall of Fame in 2006. Thelma Hopkins also found time to represent Ireland in squash. In her career, she represented six different international entities. None of the associated politics mattered to Hopkins, the sportswoman:

> If you play sport, you play because you love what you're doing.
> So you played hockey for Ireland, but because there was no

track or field in Ireland, automatically you then competed for what was available, which was the Great Britain team. We weren't really aware of the rows in Irish athletics; then we wouldn't have even known what the NACAI was.

MARY PETERS: OLYMPIC CHAMPION AND WORLD-RECORD BREAKER

In 1955, when Thelma Hopkins won the NIWAAA pentathlon title with a British-record score of 4,289 points, with Maeve Kyle in second place, a young 16-year-old Mary Peters finished a distant third. Seventeen years later, in 1972, Mary Peters stood on top of the podium in Munich, the newly crowned Olympic pentathlon champion who had given a stunning world record-breaking performance.

Peters was born in Halewood, on the outskirts of Liverpool, on 6 July 1939 and moved to Portadown in Northern Ireland in 1950, then to Belfast in 1957 following the death of her mother and the subsequent emigration of her father to Australia. Unusually for a native of Liverpool, Peters, the self-confessed atheist, did not have a 'single drop of Irish blood' in her veins as all four of her grandparents were English.

The 1955 NIWAAA Championship marked Peters' debut as a pentathlete and in 1958 she made an unimpressive Empire Games debut in Cardiff representing Northern Ireland. She represented Great Britain for the first time in 1961 but in 1962, coached by Buster McShane, a body builder, weightlifter, gym owner and innovative fitness expert, she improved on her pentathlon score from 3,940 to 4,586 when she finished in fifth place in the European Championships. She won the first of five successive WAAA pentathlon titles also in 1962. In the inaugural Olympic pentathlon in Tokyo in 1964, Peters finished in fourth place. She focused on the shot-put for the 1966 Commonwealth Games staged in Kingston. Guided by Buster McShane, she adopted a weight training programme and a 'hideously revolting' diet programme 'which virtually amounted to almost forced feeding' during which time she 'put on almost an additional three stone in muscular weight' in the summer of 1966. However, the best she could manage was the silver medal, to the chagrin of McShane who was also her employer since 1966. But, she reveals in *Mary P*, an important lesson was absorbed, 'until I hardened my mental approach I was always going to be the bridesmaid, the runner-up, the silver medallist, the second best'. Mary Peters was appointed captain of the British women's athletics team for the 1968 Olympic Games ('it was nothing more than a damned nuisance'), where she finished a disappointing ninth; in 1970, she won the first Commonwealth pentathlon title as well as the shot-put gold.

The adoption of the Fosbury Flop high-jump technique in 1971 was critical to her Olympic success; almost immediately her high-jump average increased from 1.67m to 1.78m and enabled her to jump a personal best in Munich. A full-time athlete in the months prior to Munich, she was awarded a Winston Churchill Scholarship that enabled her to travel to California in 1972 to enhance her preparation. California was 'heaven ... exactly the perfect time to go into full work. I had never known anything like it before. All I had to do was eat and sleep and train', she later recalled in *Mary P*. In Belfast, she often trained to the boom of bomb blasts and the rattle of rifle fire as 1972 was the bloodiest and most eventful year in the history of Northern Ireland's troubles. Part motivated by the desire 'to make people at home happy in some small way', Mary Peters displayed extraordinary levels of physical and mental fitness to capture the Olympic pentathlon title in 1972.

The omens looked promising when British team manager Arthur Gold presented her with her competition number, 111. On the opening day, she recorded personal bests in the 100m hurdles (13.29 seconds), the high jump (1.82m) and a pentathlon personal record in the shot-put (16.29m) to establish a 301-point lead over Heidemarie Rosendahl with the German's strongest and Peters' weakest events awaiting on the second day. Rosendahl, the Olympic long-jump champion, jumped to within a centimetre of her world record and closed the gap to manageable proportions for the final 200m event in which both Rosendahl (22.96 seconds) and Peters (24.08) recorded personal best times. If Mary Peters had run one-tenth of a second slower she would have lost the gold medal. It was the ultimate athletic triumph, an Olympic gold medal achieved by setting a new world record (4,801 points) during which she smoked at least one packet of cigarettes. Rosendahl did likewise. It was a remarkable victory for the Belfast woman and her extrovert, iron-willed coach. In Peters' words, McShane was a coach with 'enormous magnetism and infectious enthusiasm but modesty did not bother him overmuch and he could certainly be less than gentle on occasion'.

The days that followed were not easy for Peters. She refused an invitation to attend a reception given by British Prime Minister Edward Heath because the invitation did not include McShane. A death threat was delivered to the BBC's Munich headquarters and passed on to the athlete by her coach. Three days later, the apolitical Peters returned to Belfast ('my city, my home and the place I loved best') to a triumphant ticker-tape drive down Belfast's Royal Avenue that concluded with a reception at the City Hall.

McShane died tragically 6 months later in a car accident in Belfast. Mary Peters resolved to continue competing until the 1974 Commonwealth Games in Christchurch and made a pact with Mike Bull, who was also coached by McShane, that they would win the pentathlon and decathlon in Christchurch as a testimony to McShane's ability as a coach. They delivered on the promise and Peters and Bull emerged as the two best all-round athletes in the Commonwealth.

MAEVE KYLE: MOULD BREAKER SUPREME

Maeve Shankey, a native of Kilkenny, a graduate of Dublin University and a teacher in Alexandra College, married Sean Kyle in February 1954 and moved to Ballymena, County Antrim. The marriage to Sean Kyle and the move to Ballymena provided Maeve Shankey with the opportunity to develop a spectacular new career in athletics, in which she competed in three Olympic Games, two Commonwealth Games, two European Championships and the European Indoor Championships. At the time of her Olympic selection in 1956, she had been capped twenty-nine times in hockey, at which she was first capped against Wales on 6 March 1948. In 1955, Sean Kyle founded the Ballymena Ladies Athletics Club, primarily as a vehicle to cater for the summer recreational activities of the women of the Mid-Antrim Hockey Club.

At the time of her selection for Melbourne, Maeve Kyle was the mother of a young daughter, Shauna, and was selected to compete in a sport that was not available to women resident in the Republic of Ireland. The deep conservatism of Irish society again surfaced after Kyle's selection for Melbourne. The selection inspired the letter writers to the *Irish Times*, and vox populi articulated the viewpoint of the disgruntled. 'A sports field (or arena) is no place for a woman,' he proclaimed, 'and certainly not a Mrs.' The selection of a woman to represent Ireland 'was most unbecoming, unseemly and degrading of womenfolk. It must not be countenanced on any grounds.' The letter writer quoted an encyclical of Pope Pius XI to support the conservative viewpoint.

In 1956 Maeve Kyle became the first Irishwoman to compete in athletics at the Olympic Games and was eliminated in the first round of both the 100m and the 200m. She also represented Ireland in the same events at the Rome Games in 1960. In Tokyo (1964) she qualified for the semi-finals of both the 400m and the 800m.

Maeve Kyle is associated with many of the decisive steps that paved the way for the introduction of women's athletics in the Republic of Ireland. In 1960 she was invited by Trinity captain Colm Shillington to take a team of women athletes to compete in the College Sports; Maeve, Lorna McGarvey and Irene Larkin from the Ballymena Athletics Club competed against athletes recruited from the university's tennis and hockey clubs in the 100yd and the 4 x 100yd relay. After the event the women were greeted in the Pavilion by President of Ireland Eamon de Valera, who was an old chess-playing friend of William Thrift, Maeve Kyle's grandfather. The greeting provided tacit approval for the staging of women's athletics in the Republic of Ireland and organisers of Dublin athletics meets cautiously began to include women's races in their programmes. The Cork City Sports of 5 July 1960 also staged a 100yd race for women in which Mary and Phyllis Jefford of the Hilltown AC and B. Lyons, Etie Buckley and Marjorie and Evelyn Kenny, all of St Aloysius School, competed. On 2 July 1963, Maeve Kyle, 'looking like a Goddess', according to one who was there, competed in the Cork City Sports where a Munster Ladies' 100yd championship and a 220yd ladies' handicap race were included on the programme. Kyle comfortably beat the Jefford sisters in both events.

She returned in 1964 to compete, this time accompanied by Lorna McGarvey, in what proved to be a controversial appearance when Jack Crump, secretary of the BAAB, was alerted to their competing. 'They have rendered themselves ineligible for international competition under IAAF rules,' Crump announced, and Kyle and McGarvey were prevented from competing in an international meet at the White City. The problem was the Cork City Sports were promoted by the NACAI, an organisation suspended from the IAAF. Maeve Kyle had an answer to this: the NACAI had no women's organisation and therefore it would have been impossible to compete under its jurisdiction, and the two athletes had received permission from the NIWAAA to compete in Cork. The matter was quickly resolved and the NIWAAA ruled that the athletes had competed 'unwittingly' in Cork; as a result no offence was committed. Maeve Kyle and Lorna McGarvey were reinstated in time to represent Ireland in the international against Scotland staged in Ayr in August 1964.

FIRST INTERNATIONAL

Six weeks after the Cork City Sports, the first international match to feature women was staged at Santry on 15 August 1963 when Belgium competed against Ireland for the first time. The welcoming party at Dublin Airport included Maeve Kyle and Mary Barry. Seven women featured on the Ireland team (the majority from the NIAAA): Jacqueline Spence, Joan Atkinson, Lorna McGarvey, Mary Barry, Mary Peters, Maeve Kyle and Thelma Hopkins. Their inclusion produced a far closer contest than was anticipated as Joan Atkinson won the 100yd; Hopkins won the 80yd hurdles after a great duel with Mary Peters; McGarvey and Kyle dominated the 220yd and they also trumped Belgium in the 4 x 110yd relay (Kyle, Peters, McGarvey, Atkinson).

A. Reilly, C. Love, Gay Porter, Hazel Tennyson, Jacqueline Spence, Lorna McGarvey, Maeve Kyle, P. Holbrook, Peggy Hogan, Rosemary Reilly and Thelma Hopkins featured in the next international against Scotland staged at Ayr on 8 August 1964. In this full women's international, Scotland emerged victorious (66–51). Women enjoyed a third international outing in September in the triangular meet with Belgium and Scotland staged in Brussels, where a double win by Peters in the shot-put and high jump secured an Irish victory. This Ireland team included Maeve Kyle and Mary Peters and the intricate political situation associated with Irish athletics was clearly illustrated a month later when Maeve Kyle competed in her third Olympic Games representing Ireland and Mary Peters made her Olympic debut representing Great Britain.

FIRST CHAMPIONSHIPS

At the NACAI Congress of 1966 two motions were passed, one calling for a women's national cross-country championship, the other for a committee to draw up an All-Ireland track-and-field championship programme. A precedent had been set in February 1966 when a women's cross-country race was staged prior to the Munster senior men's cross-country championship held at Carrigaline, County Cork. Also in 1966, the Munster NACAI Championships included two women's championships on the programme (100yd and 880yd); the Cork County Championships also included a single championship race for women (100yd). Ironically, the women's cross-country championship approved at the 1966 Congress was the last championship event staged under the auspices of the NACAI prior to its dissolution. In 1967, following the formation of BLE, Bishop Cornelius Lucey granted permission for the establishment of a separate women's county board in Cork for the promotion of women's athletics, and this survived until 1970 when it was felt that women's athletics no longer needed separate representation.

Women were included in the AAUE National Championship programme for the first time in June 1965 when eleven events were staged, and fittingly Maeve Kyle was one of the athletes to win a national title. Claire Dowling of Clonliffe Harriers won the 220yd, the 440yd and long jump treble as did Rosemary Reilly (Crusaders) in the shot, javelin and discus; Hazel Tennison in the 880yd and Peggy Hogan in the mile were middle-distance winners representing Crusaders and Jacqueline Spence of the same club won the 100yd title. A year later, Hogan became the first Irish women's cross-country champion. In June 1981, the first official marathon championship for women was held in Cork and was won by Carey May.

WOMEN RACE AHEAD

Since breaking the men-only mould, women have been integrated to athletics on an equal-status footing more than in any other sport in the country. The establishment of BLE and BLOE and the introduction of schools' championships for girls in 1970 were important in reducing the barriers to participation. State legislation also contributed, as did policies and funding aimed at increasing women's participation in sports introduced by the various semi-state bodies responsible for promoting sport in Ireland.

Women's progress in the sport since 1970 has been remarkable. Ten men had walked on the moon and at least one Russian woman had travelled in space before a woman resident in the Republic of Ireland represented Ireland in athletics in the Olympic Games. This situation ended in 1972 when Margaret Murphy, Mary Treacy and Claire Walshe were included in the team of thirteen athletes that competed in Munich. The inclusion of Walshe, one of the true pioneers of women's athletics in Ireland, was particularly appropriate. A member of Clonliffe Harriers, she won the club's first race for women, a 600yd gallop down Santry Avenue, held on 17 December 1963; in the European Championships, at Helsinki (1971), she became the first woman resident in the Republic of Ireland to qualify for a European final, in which she finished in sixth place. In 1984, Caroline O'Shea became the first Irishwoman to qualify for an Olympic track-and-field final (800m); Patricia Walsh, a scholarship student at the University of Tennessee, qualified for the discus final and became the first (and is still the only) Irishwoman to qualify for an Olympic throwing final. Since then, the women Olympians have outperformed the men by qualifying for ten finals compared to seven for the men.

The structure of the Irish athletics team dramatically shifted for the London Olympic Games. Women outnumbered their male counterparts on a 2:1 ratio (14–7) and were also in the majority at Rio. As previously documented, Sonia O'Sullivan became Ireland's second track medallist in Sydney and Olive Loughnane and Derval O'Rourke have won world titles; Catherina McKiernan won four successive silver medals in the World Cross-Country Championships (1991–1995) as well as the European title in 1995 along with running the fastest debut marathon by a woman when winning in Berlin (1997) and becoming the first Irish runner to win the London Marathon (1998). The remarkable Michelle Walshe won her first Irish sprint titles in 1977 at the age of 15 years and 361 days and ended her championship winning career in 1995 with a triple success at 100, 200 and 400m distances to bring her total of national titles to thirty-one, the greatest number of such titles by an Irish woman athlete. The great Waterford all-round athlete Kelly Proper has seventeen outdoor and nineteen indoor national titles to her credit in sprinting, long jumping and pentathlon-heptathlon events.

The growth of recreational running and mass-participation events has been extraordinary. 'The Women of Ireland are running and you know neither the day nor the hour when as you turn a corner you'll be trampled all over by dainty feet,' Con Houlihan wrote. Nowhere is this more evident than in the Women's Mini-Marathon held annually in Dublin on the June Bank Holiday weekend. It has grown from its not-so-humble beginnings in 1983 with almost 9,000 participants to a staggering 41,006 women's world-record field in 2014. Since 1983, nearly 992,000 women have entered the event, raising an estimated €203 million for various charities in the process.

SONIA O'SULLIVAN: THE PERFECT IRISH HERO

The achievements of Sonia O'Sullivan have been dotted throughout this book but it is appropriate that they be documented as a unit to illustrate the magnificence of a career without equal in the modern history of Irish athletics. In 2012, Sonia O'Sullivan became the first Irishwoman to hold the position of *chef de mission* of Team Ireland at the Summer Games. This completed a magnificent portfolio of Olympic accomplishment by the athlete, who told the *Irish Runner* in June 1986, 'Ultimately like all athletes, I would love to compete in and win a medal at the Olympic Games'. It was an ambition that was accomplished several times over. A competitor at the Games of 1992, 1996, 2000 and 2004, a five-times finalist, a silver medallist at Sydney where she also carried the Irish flag at the opening ceremony and an executive member of the Olympic Council of Ireland, she was honoured with the responsibility of lighting the Olympic Cauldron in St Stephen's Green, Dublin as the final participant of the Torch Relay when it visited Dublin in 2012.

In 1987, Sonia O'Sullivan again told RTE's Brendan O'Reilly that she would like to run in the Olympics, when she won her first Irish cross-country title as a 17-year-old, in what Dick Hooper writing in the *Irish Runner* described as 'far and away the shock of the day' before adding that 'rarely has there been such a display of raw talent at this level'. The raw talent was quickly refined and the promise fulfilled.

A scholarship to Villanova followed in the autumn and after a difficult transition she settled to win five NCAA individual titles. In 1991, in Sheffield, she became the first athlete since Ronnie Delany to win a gold medal in the World University Championships (1,500m), and she also won a silver medal in the 3,000m. These were the first medals in what became an extraordinary collection of thirteen individual major championship medals that also included an Olympic silver medal (2000), a World Championship gold (1995) and silver (1993), three European gold (1994 (1), 1998) and two silver medals (2002), two world cross-country gold medals (1998) and a silver World Indoor Championship medal (1997). Following the 2000 Olympics, O'Sullivan made her marathon debut, winning the Dublin marathon in a time of 2:35:42 on 30 October. In April 2005, O'Sullivan ran the London Marathon for the first time and finished eighth in a personal best time of 2:29:01. She also established two world records. In 1991, at Boston, she set a new world indoor 5,000m record of 15:176.28 and in 1994 in Edinburgh she established a world 2,000m record (5:25.36). No Irish athlete has a record that is remotely comparable, but there were the occasional setbacks and it was this combination, as Paul Rouse has written in *Sport and Ireland*, that 'conspired to make her the perfect Irish hero: fragile and raw and a winner but not too much a winner'.

12

THE USA SCHOLARSHIP SCENE

IN THE BEGINNING ...

Irish athletics was rescued from international isolation by the American scholarship system. The trail began in London in 1948 with the superb performance of Jimmy Reardon in the 400m at the Olympic Games, which alerted USA officials to Irish athletics talent. In London, Riordan chatted to two American athletes, George Guida and Browning Ross, who were students at Villanova. Jimmy Reardon was attracted by the possibilities of life in America and in 1949 he became Ireland's first scholarship athlete when he enrolled in Villanova. The Villanova Pipeline, as the trail of Irish athletes to the Pennsylvanian college became known, was activated.

Cumin Clancy, who competed in the discus at the London Games, was the next Irish athlete recruited to Villanova and, in February 1950, John Joe Barry enrolled. The achievements of the next recruit, Ronnie Delany, proved that the American college system worked and his victory at Melbourne provided the foundation for a new middle-distance running tradition in Ireland. The centrality of America to Delany's victory with its uber-competitive system, its quality coaching and an environment where the cultivation of excellence was the norm, was acknowledged by the Olympic champion. In a *Sports Illustrated* feature in 1968, Delaney explained:

There is no doubt in my mind that I would not have won an Olympic title if I had remained in Ireland. I benefited and developed under the expert tuition of Jumbo Elliott. I learned tactical sense from my many skirmishes on the board tracks. And above all I competed against the best competition available week after week, year after year, throughout the USA ...

Over 30 years after Delany's victory, Frank O'Mara offered a similar testimonial, in an *Irish Runner* interview, after landing his first world indoor title in 1986:

If you're Irish and you want to make it to the top in athletics, you have to come out here [USA]. You can't do it at home. There's just no way, for many, many reasons. At home, you don't have the weather, you don't have the facilities, you don't have the competition, and you don't rub up against people who are just out to win. America is win, win, win.

Delany's Olympic victory introduced the magical name of Villanova and coach Jumbo Elliott to the Irish public, and the Villanova Pipeline became part of the culture of Irish athletics. Noel Carroll, Frank Murphy, Eamonn Coghlan, Marcus O'Sullivan, Gerry O'Reilly, John Hartnett, Donie Walsh and Sonia O'Sullivan followed the Villanova trail and prospered athletically. The most recent Villanova recruit, Síofra Cléirigh Büttner, in April 2017 ran crucial legs in all three of the distance relays at the Penn Relays as Villanova won all three events (distance relay, 4 x 800m and 4 x 1,500m) for the sixth time in the college's history. Sonia O'Sullivan made a similar contribution in 1991. Cléirigh Büttner is part of a long tradition; in 1994, to commemorate the 100th anniversary of the relays, sixteen Wall of Famers including Eamonn Coghlan and Ronnie Delany were honoured. Delany was undefeated in 3 years of Penn competition and helped to set five meet records; Coghlan was a nine-time winner at Penn and was involved in three meet records.

   In the 1950s and 1960s, opportunities for second-level education in Ireland were limited to the better-off members of society while university education was an even rarer privilege. The bartering of athletics talent for college (university) education was an attractive proposition for the athletically talented and several Irish athletes availed of the opportunity. Brendan O'Reilly, who established new standards of excellence in Irish high jumping, was in his mid-20s when he became a student at the University of Michigan in 1954, the year he set a new national high-jump record of 1.97m (6' 5¾") and won the AAA title (1.95m), which opened the doors to the university in Ann Arbor. There, on 25 February 1956, he jumped 2.02m (6' 7½"), a performance that comfortably reached the required standard of 1.98m (6' 6") set by the Olympic Council of Ireland for Olympic selection. Unfortunately, Donore Harriers were unable to finance O'Reilly's trip to Melbourne.

John Lawlor was another mature student who prospered in the American system. Lawlor began hammer throwing when he joined *An Garda Síochána* in 1953 and in September 1956 became a scholarship athlete at Boston University. Prompted by Brendan O'Reilly, Lawlor contacted American colleges and outlined his athletic credentials. Three responded with offers of scholarships. The reputation of hammer coach Ed Flanagan attracted Lawlor to Boston University where he made spectacular progress. In 1958, he became the first Irish hammer thrower to break the 200' barrier (60.96m) and won three successive NCAA hammer titles (1958–1960). The Olympic year began well for Lawlor. He extended his Irish record to 64.60m (211' 11") as well as winning the NCAA title with 63.76m (209' 2"). Prior to the Olympic Games, he produced the best throw of his career with an effort of 65.18m (213' 10") at Bakersfield, California on 24 June 1960 at the US Championships. Lawlor qualified for the Olympic final in Rome and a throw of 64.95m (213' 1") secured him fourth place in an extraordinary final in which the first eight throwers broke the Olympic record set in Melbourne by Hal Connolly.

The reputation of a coach was a major influencing factor in deciding on an athlete's destination of choice, although this was not always what it seemed to be. Fanahan McSweeney became the first Irishman to accept an athletics scholarship to McNeese State College in Louisiana. He was attracted there by the warm weather and the presence of Bob Hayes on the college's coaching staff. He arrived to discover that this Bob Hayes was not the Olympic 100m champion of 1968 but a field events coach. Undeterred, he stayed on and brought Irish 400m running to new levels. Brendan O'Reilly facilitated the athletics scholarship to Louisiana. In February 1970, in the final of the USA indoor 400m, at the Houston Astrodome, he finished a close second to Fred Newhouse (USA). His time of 46.3 seconds (without using starting blocks) was inside Tommie Smith's old world record and was a new European record for the 400m and 440yd.

JACK O'RIORDAN KILLS THE FATTED CALF

In 1956, Tom O'Riordan became the first Kerry man to win the Irish Schools' 1-mile championship and did so in a record time of 4:35.1. Post-Leaving Certificate employment with the Tralee Town Council followed, but the young O'Riordan harboured ambitions of becoming an Olympic athlete, a dream that was unlikely to come true in the relative isolation of north Kerry. A newspaper article in which the American ambassador advised aspiring Irish athletes to acquire a copy of the *Directory of American Colleges* encouraged O'Riordan to explore the possibility of obtaining an athletics scholarship to the USA. Letters were written to twelve colleges, and officials of the Idaho State College, Pocatello, Idaho responded offering a scholarship commencing in September 1957. Jack O'Riordan sold two of his prize cattle to finance the air ticket and his son Tom flew from Shannon via Detroit, Denver and Salt Lake City and arrived in Pocatello on 15 October 1957. O'Riordan's athletics world was transformed by the scholarship. Instead of running laps of the triangular field known as the *cúilín* opposite the family farm at Tubrid crossroads near Ardfert, County Kerry, he was exposed to the latest coaching methodologies and the intense competitive world of the American collegiate system. In his first year he travelled across the USA to compete in exotic locations such as Fargo, Boise, Provo, Denver, Bismarck, Sioux Falls, Lincoln, Wichita, Des Moines, Santa Fe and Sacramento.

The move to Idaho State, with its high-altitude location, and a wonderfully warm relationship with a great coach and father figure, Milton Holt, transformed O' Riordan into an international-class athlete. He managed only a single trip home during his time in the USA but coped with the homesickness and isolation. This trip was in the summer of 1959, when he won the mile, the 1,500m and 2-mile NACAI titles. He was promptly suspended by the American AAU for competing in events organised by an organisation not recognised by the IAAF.

Tom O'Riordan spent the summer of 1960 in San José, California where he was part of Hungarian Mihaly Igloi's coaching group. Igloi coached two of the great Hungarian middle-distance runners of the 1950s, Lásló Tábori and Sándor Iharos, who fled to the USA after the Hungarian Uprising of 1956. Here O'Riordan was introduced to Igloi's punishing and meticulously planned interval training sessions, which were designed to overcome physical and mental pain barriers.

O'Riordan returned to Ireland where his USA-built reservoir of fitness and knowledge propelled him to a superb 1963 season. He established nine Irish records and in June 1964 recorded a best time of 13:18.4 for the 3 miles at Santry Stadium, one of the fastest in the world for the year, and an Irish record that survived until 1972. He represented Ireland in the 5,000m at the Tokyo Olympic Games.

THE PIPELINE IS EXTENDED ...

The trickle of athletes to the USA became a stream in the late 1960s and continued unhindered until the mid-1990s. In 1987, between 100 and 110 athletes were on scholarships in forty-one colleges across the length and breadth of the USA. Villanova was strongly challenged as the destination of choice for Irish athletes as other colleges identified Irish talent and became identifiably Irish. In 1968, East Tennessee State University coach Dave Walker, advised by Brendan O'Reilly, recruited Michael Heery to Johnson City and began a strong Irish association with the college; over forty Irish athletes have since attended the college, including two-time Olympians Neil Cusack, Eddie Leddy and Ray Flynn. In 1972, Cusack won the NCAA cross-country individual title and the college team known as the Irish Brigade finished second in the NCAA Cross-Country Championships. Fred Dwyer, a Villanova graduate, became head coach at Manhattan College and recruited numerous Irish athletes to the New York college. In 1973, John McDonnell travelled to Ireland on the advice of Ronnie Long and began to recruit to the University of Arkansas. In 1981, Carey May became one of the first Irish woman scholarship athletes and was recruited by the high-altitude Brigham Young University where she became one of the leading marathon runners in the world.

Some graduates of the scholarship system made the successful transition to the coach's office and married their knowledge of the Irish educational and athletics systems to their American college experience to produce a skill set that few coaches could offer. Mick

Byrne, a graduate of Providence, became an assistant coach at Iona before becoming head coach in 1989. Ray Treacy, a scholarship athlete at Providence College, Rhode Island became head coach in Providence in 1984. The native of Villierstown, County Waterford has used his Irish connections to recruit talented Irish runners to the Rhode Island school and, of these, Marie McMahon, Sinead Delahunty, Mark Carroll, Maria McCambridge, Rosin McGettigan, Martin Fagan and Stephanie Reilly have represented Ireland in Olympic competition. Marcus O'Sullivan, whose athletic accomplishments are found dotted through this book, has been the head coach at Villanova since 1998.

JOHN MCDONNELL, AMERICA'S MOST SUCCESSFUL COLLEGE COACH

John McDonnell was born in Crossmolina, County Mayo on 2 July 1938, and became involved in athletics in his late teens as he competed in local sports meets in his native county. Ronnie Delany's victory in Melbourne provided one of the defining moments in McDonnell's life. 'He was my idol before he won that medal. I started to get interested because of him, but when he won that gold medal that's when I decided I had to go to America,' he explained in his autobiography, *John McDonnell*. He moved to Dublin in 1958, joined the Clonliffe Harriers Athletics Club and progressed from running local sports meets in Mayo to competing in the national senior championships where he finished in second place in the AAU 3-mile Championship in 1960 before winning the 1-mile title in 1962 and 1963. He emigrated to the USA in November 1963 and, after a holding a variety of jobs in New York, he landed an athletics scholarship to the University of Southern Louisiana at Lafayette. He graduated in 1970 and returned to the east coast, but a year later he went back to Lafayette to a teaching post. A third move followed when he was appointed coach to the University of Arkansas cross-country programme. He chose this as the Arkansas countryside and the Ozark Mountains reminded him of his native County Mayo.

In his spiritual home, John McDonnell's journey to becoming the most successful athletics coach in American college history began. He inherited a system that was unsupported, unstructured and underfunded. Arkansas finished second last at the 1971 South

Western Conference Cross-Country Championship and the college scored a single point in the 1972 Conference Track Championship. Arkansas had nothing to offer athletes with potential and initially the coach had difficulty in getting high-school students to even discuss the possibilities of joining the university. In his first season, he recruited two athletes to the Arkansas programme, including his first Irish athlete, Desmond O'Connor, who after a year moved on to Angelo State in Texas.

Unable to attract USA athletes and with a minimal budget, John McDonnell travelled to Ireland in the summer of 1973 and recruited the future Olympian Niall O'Shaughnessy, as a miler, although the Adare athlete had never raced the distance, Tom Aspel from Waterford, Derek Reilly from Dublin and Steve Barr from Essex to add to his lone American recruit.

McDonnell was soon successful. Arkansas failed to win the South-Western Conference Cross-Country Championship in 1973 but the Razorbacks would never lose another conference championship during the McDonnell era. Instead, the college went on to win thirty-four consecutive titles from 1974 to 2008. Niall O'Shaughnessy became McDonnell's first All-American athlete when he finished in sixth place at the NCAA Indoor Championships in the 880yd. He was the first Arkansas athlete to earn the distinction in 20 years and was also the first of twenty-three Olympians coached by McDonnell from the USA, Canada, Bermuda, Zambia, Australia and Ireland. Paul Donovan, Frank O'Mara, Niall Bruton and Alistair Cragg were the other Irish Olympians benefiting from the Mayo man's experience. 'John was a total influence on me through his coaching abilities. I would give him full credit for my success,' O'Shaughnessy later acknowledged.

John McDonnell retired in 2008 as the most successful coach in the history of American intercollegiate sport. During his time, he amassed an astonishing total of forty national championships (eleven cross-country, nineteen indoor and ten outdoor track-and-field titles), the most by any coach in any sport in NCAA history. He also guided Arkansas teams to five Triple Crown (the cross-country, indoor and outdoor track titles in a single year) victories and eight successive track-and-field titles (1992–1999). McDonnell's Razorbacks also won eighty-three conference titles and twelve consecutive NCAA indoor championships, the longest streak of national titles by any college, in any sport, in NCAA history. He also coached forty-four individual national champions to 100 national titles.

PHILIP CONWAY: THE RETURNING EVANGELIST

Philip Conway availed of an athletics scholarship to Boston University in 1966. He graduated in physical education and returned to Ireland in 1970, where he began a teaching career in Rockwell College. He returned to Boston in 1971 and enrolled in a postgraduate course in Springfield College. He represented Ireland in the shot-put in 1972 at the Munich Games, where he performed at less than his best, but the spin-off from his American involvement was to have immense significance for the future development of Irish athletics.

Philip Conway's return to Ireland from the USA in 1973 was one of the most significant events in Irish athletics during the decade. He immediately saw the need to revive the culture of hammer and weight throwing in a country where the activity was virtually dead. Since 1948, only John Lawlor and Conway had represented Ireland in Olympic competition. John Lawlor was accorded legendary status in Boston but was virtually unknown in Ireland. Only two modern tungsten hammers were available in the country. At the end of 1975, in the all-time ranking list of Irish hammer throwers, only eight of the top thirty-five throws were recorded during the 1970s. In the list of September 1979, thirteen of the thirty best throws belonged to the 1970s and seven of the top-ten throws were thrown from 1977 to 1979. A remarkable transformation in hammer throwing had occurred.

The development of niches of excellence is one of the defining characteristics of modern Irish athletics. Pockets of specialism have emerged, inspired by wise leadership and the interests and coaching expertise of dedicated individuals. The emergence of a number of international-class throwing athletes in the 1980s is one such development, partly inspired by institutional interventions that included the establishment of BLOE in 1970 and the introduction of hammer throwing to schools' athletics championships. The Bears coaching courses, held in Gormanston College, County Meath at Christmas and Easter, which brought together athletes and coaches from all associations for training and coaching, also played a part. Links with the British Hammer Circle enabled cross-fertilisation of expertise to occur. Teachers with a passion for athletics also enthusiastically promoted throwing amongst their students. These included Dan Kennedy, a PE teacher at Wesley College (Dublin), who introduced in-depth video analysis to the equation; Fr Michael Lavelle in Rockwell College, Tipperary; Pat Creagh who travelled from Dublin to the Cistercian College, Roscrea, County Tipperary twice weekly to coach athletics; Jim Byrne at Blackrock College and Philip Conway, who became a PE teacher in Belvedere College after he completed his studies in the USA. A platform was created, a trickle of talented young throwers emerged, meaningful competitions were available and a new coterie of athletes were able to target realistic athletic and career goals.

Philip Conway was mainly responsible for establishing the school for throwers that assembled every Saturday morning at the UCD campus at Belfield. Conway's own career path enabled him to present a vision of attainable athletic and educational goals to young athletes that were complementary. Throwing excellence provided an opportunity for career advancement by means of athletics scholarships, and at least thirty-five throwers travelled to the USA on athletics scholarships over a 20-year period from the mid-1970s. Throwers became a significant presence on Irish Olympic teams between 1980 and 2000 and the law of unintended consequences also kicked in. The availability of weight-event athletes, with their explosive power, provided ideal drivers and brakemen for the Ireland bobsleigh teams that competed in the Winter Games in 1992, 1998 and 2002.

The UCD-based Saturday initiative played a central role in the promotion of a culture of throwing excellence and students from several schools availed of the coaching and training opportunity. The evangelist Conway wrote to over fifty schools to recruit as many potential throwers as possible. The annual Hammerama midwinter festival, organised in association with Crusaders AC, developed into one of the athletics highlights of the Irish season and attained a championship-like status. In the inaugural festival in 1973, nineteen throwers competed, but the 1978 festival attracted an entry of sixty including eight throwers from the UK youth squad. The Irish Hammermania Association was formed in 1975 with a mission to increase the number of participants throughout the country, to improve the all-round standard of performance, to provide more competitive opportunities and to incentivise young throwers to continue into senior ranks.

During this period, the Irish record book was rewritten for throwing events, with the records established still standing: in 1970 Conway himself with a throw of 51.08m broke Cummin Clancy's long-standing discus record (46.49m) set at the Penn Relays in 1951; in the 1990s Nick Sweeney (Harvard College) set nine separate records and moved the record from 58.46m to its present 67.89m between 1991 and 1998. On 23 July 1978, Sean Egan surpassed John Lawlor's Irish hammer record with a throw of 65.56m (215' 1") and improved on this mark on four occasions. Declan Hegarty set seven national records between April 1983 and April 1985. Hegarty's best throw of 77.80m has yet to be surpassed. Four more hammer throwers, all American scholarship athletes – Roman Linscheid, Declan Hegarty, Conor McCullough and Paddy McGrath – represented Ireland in Olympic competition between 1984 and 2000. The shot-put record of 20.04m established by Paul Quirke in New York on 7 July 1992 was the sixth such record established in a matter of weeks. Quirke was the first and is still the only Irish thrower to break the 20m barrier for the shot. Terry McHugh was not a scholarship athlete but was part of the UCD group and became an international-class javelin thrower. McHugh dominated the event like no other athlete in any event and established seventeen national records between 1982 and 2000, winning an extraordinary twenty-one successive national titles (1984–2004).

NCAA CHAMPIONS

Only a small number of Irish athletes have succeeded in winning NCAA titles despite the wealth of Irish athletics talent that passed through the American college system. The first Irish athlete to win an NCAA title was Ronnie Delany in 1956 in the 1,500m; he defended it in 1957 before doing the 'Delany Double' by winning the 1 mile (4:03.5) and 880yd (1:48.5) titles in 1958 in Berkeley, California, within 45 minutes of each other. A year earlier in Austin, Texas he almost completed the same double when he won the mile (4:06.5) and 35 minutes later finished second in the 880yd in a new national record time (1:47.8). Truly extraordinary performances by an extraordinary athlete. Delany's four titles are a record for an Irish athlete.

John Lawlor (Boston University), the only field-event athlete to win a title, was next to crack the NCAA code and he won NCAA hammer titles in 1959 and 1960. Eamonn Coghlan was the next to succeed and won successive titles in 1975 (1 mile) and 1976 (1,500m). Frank O'Mara won the 1,500m title (1983), Sean Dollman the 10,000m (1992), and Alistair Craig the 5,000m title in 2003 and the 10,000m title in 2004. Dollman and Craig were South African-born athletes who declared for Ireland. In cross-country Neil Cusack (1972), Dollman (1991) and Keith Kelly (2000) were title winners. Drogheda-native Kelly was the last Irish (or British) athlete to win the title. A student at Providence College, Kelly suffered numerous injuries that eventually ended his competitive running career after he won the Irish National Cross-Country Championship in 2009.

The first Irish woman to win an NCAA title was Valerie McGovern who won the 5,000m title in 1989 and defended it in 1990 in addition to winning the indoor 5,000m title. Sonia O'Sullivan won the first of her two successive 3,000m track and cross-country titles in 1990 and in 1991 she achieved the Triple Crown of titles, winning the 3,000m indoor title also. Mary Cullen (Providence College) is the third Irish female athlete to secure an NCAA championship, having done so in 2006 in the 5,000m.

Valerie McGovern's experience of the scholarship circuit is instructive as it includes the uncertainties and athletic and educational possibilities involved. McGovern dreamed of following in the footsteps of Eamonn Coghlan and John Treacy and furthering her athletics career in the USA, but no offers were tabled when she finished her secondary education. She was on a working holiday on the Greek Islands when the dream offer came. One of her club coaches had secured a post at the Austin Peay State University in Tennessee and planned on building his women's cross-country team around McGovern. She accepted the offer and joined the eclectic mix of athletes that constituted the embryonic women's programme at Peay which was abandoned within a year. Fortunately, McGovern's dream did not become a nightmare as in 1988 the University of Kentucky offered the Dublin athlete a full scholarship and she became one of the college's athletics stars. She also prospered academically and the student who never studied science in her Irish school earned a Bachelor of Science in dietetics, a Master of Science in nutritional biochemistry and a doctorate in nutritional sciences in the college that became her second home.

ANOTHER WAY ...

Adjusting to the American college system did not come easy. Cross-country competition, with races on most weekends, dominates the autumn season and continues into mid-December; indoor competition begins in January and the track season runs from April until early June. The intense competition with its associated heavy training workload, the travel, the culture shock, the scholastic demands and the homesickness were complicating factors. The USA college sports' system is a result-driven business and a coach's tenure in office depends on the performance of his chosen athletes. In an article in *Runner's World* in August 1987, Brother John Dooley divided Irish scholarship athletes into four categories. The winners who 'had periods of home-sickness, injury, doubt, struggle and even disillusion, but because of their inherent qualities they have overcome and achieved international acclaim'. Eamonn Coghlan, for example, abandoned the Villanova experiment after 6 months and only the intervention of his girlfriend Yvonne forced his return to the college. The scorers formed the second group and constituted the majority of athletes availing of scholarships, 'they have a positive experience of the system and 'appreciate the educational, sporting, and career opportunities American has offered'. The third group were those who failed to adapt to the difficult challenges of the new environment. 'They spend their whole time injured, imagining they are injured, dodging, deceiving or making excuses.' The final small group were those 'who have used the scholarship as a way of escaping the hum-drum life of home or to get away for a good time or to get a free third-level education'.

Unhappiness at what was perceived as a drain of athletics talent occupied the thoughts of athletics officials, but it wasn't until the mid-1980s that an alternative system was available to talented Irish athletes. Inspired by the innovative Dr Tony O'Neill, University College Dublin began to offer sports scholarships and Noel Carroll provided the coaching expertise.

Noel Carroll personified the athletic and educational value of the athletics scholarship. A native of Annagassan, County Louth, he worked as a farm labourer and builder's labourer after leaving school at 13 years of age. He joined the Irish Army as a private in 1959, a decision motivated by the opportunities he believed army life offered to develop as an athlete. Carroll, as a young boy, was 'foolish enough to believe that [he] would be the next Irish runner to reach Villanova after Delany' and his obsession with running around the fields of Annagassan earned him a reputation as the village eccentric. In 1961, Carroll joined the Villanova trail as the fifth scholarship athlete from Ireland accepted at the famous finishing school for Irish athletes. He prospered at Villanova and twice won the outstanding athlete award at the Penn Relays (1964–1965). In 1963, he ranked fourth in the world in the 800m, set a European 880yd record and won his first AAA title. In 1964, he was part of a Villanova quartet that set a world 4 x 880yd record but the Olympic Games in Tokyo were a bitter disappointment as he failed to reproduce his USA form. Noel Carroll added two more 880yd AAA titles to his collection in 1966 and 1968 and won three successive European indoor 800m titles (1966–1968). Unfortunately, in Mexcio, he failed again to reproduce his form and was eliminated from the opening heats of the 400m and 800m.

Other universities followed the example of UCD and in 2006, the Dublin City University (DCU) Sports Academy Scholarship programme was launched and was dedicated to providing top Irish sportspeople with an opportunity to train and compete at the highest level while getting a top academic qualification.

In 2014, only six Irish athletes became scholarship athletes in the USA. In 2015, females outnumbered the males for the first time as six male and ten female athletes enrolled in American colleges. A total of forty-three athletes are currently on athletics scholarships in the USA. The changed circumstances were reflected in the Irish team that competed in the 2016 Rio Olympic Games where only one of the Irish-born athletes, Michelle Finn, a graduate of Western Kentucky, was an American-scholarship athlete.

13

MORE MILESTONES

1873: The first Irish athletics championships were held on 7 July 1873 at College Park, Dublin. Matthew M. Stritch of the RIC Club achieved a treble in the thirteen-event championships, Tom Davin recorded a world-best high jump (1.78m) and *Dracula* author, Bram Stoker was a judge in the 7-mile walking event. The IAAF's centenary history acknowledged Ireland 'as the nation with the longest unbroken sequence of National Championships'.

1876: The first international match in the history of athletics was held on 5 June 1876 at Lansdowne Road, Dublin with England and Ireland in opposition. England did not contest the hammer throw, the first event scheduled, and conceded the event to Maurice Davin who also won the weight putting event; Tom Davin won the high jump from his brother Pat as Ireland scored victories in four of the first five events staged. This ended the Irish victory sequence and England achieved a 9-4 victory in the first international in athletics history.

1895: A series of annual international matches (the first of their kind in the sport) between Ireland and Scotland began at Central Park, Glasgow on 20 July 1895 and continued unbroken until 1913. England was included in 1914 before the meet was abandoned for the First World War years. The series was revived in 1920 and continued until 1932 and for most of this time also included England.

1922: On 9 June 1922, the remarkable J.J. Keane was elected as the first member in Ireland of the International Olympic Committee. The farmer's son from Lackendarragh, County Limerick, a winner of two All-Ireland football medals with Dublin (1899, 1900) and a founder member of both the Irish Olympic Council (1920) and the NACAI, became the first commoner to be accepted into the royal family of international sport.

1924: The Tailteann Games were held daily from 2 August 1924 until the closing ceremony on Sunday 17 August. Over 5,000 competitors took part (3,070 in the Paris Olympics), across twenty-five different categories of events, based primarily on the Olympic model. Motorcycle racing, speedboat racing, aeroplane races, horse racing and billiards were included but athletics was the dominant sport. The games were also held in 1928 and 1932 after which they were abandoned. The 1932 games were a non-event and any chance of saving the games was ended when the NACAI opted out of the IAAF.

1931: The International Cross-Country Championships were held at the Baldoyle Racecourse, Dublin on 28 March 1931. Tim Smythe, a founder member of the O'Callaghan's Mills Club in County Clare, honoured the occasion by becoming the first Irish winner of the championships and finished over 100yd ahead of English runner-up, J.W. Winfield, in a time of 48:52.19.

1932: The Homecoming. Nothing in Irish sport compares to the return to Dublin of the Olympic champions Bob Tisdall and Dr Pat O'Callaghan on 27 August 1932 as over 250,000 people poured onto the streets of Dublin in a spontaneous demonstration of welcome and celebration. The triumphal procession began in Dun Laoghaire and halted at the RDS for a musical recital. A civic reception was held at the Mansion House and the extravaganza of marching bands and athletes concluded at the Gresham Hotel where an official banquet was held that brought together politicians with irreconcilable differences to pay their respects to the nation's heroes. It included Eamon de Valera, W.T. Cosgrave, the Belfast nationalist MP Joe Devlin, as well as representatives of the Diplomatic Corps.

1948: The Irish Olympic Council forwarded the entries of athletes to the London organising committee nominated by the NACAI and the

AAUE without signing the entry forms as required by the Olympic Charter. The entry of the AAUE athletes was accepted by the IOC at a special session while the NACAI athletes were rejected. As a result, ten Irish athletes competed at the London Games but their performances are ignored in the Official Report of the Irish Olympic Council.

1952: The IOC rejected the Irish athletes nominated by the AAUE to compete in the Helsinki Games. As a result, officials of the AAUE contacted E.J. Holt, honorary general secretary of the IAAF who made representations to the President of the IOC, Sigfrid Edström, who immediately contacted the organising committee in Helsinki and ordered them to accept the entries submitted by the AAUE. As a result, Paul Dolan and Joe West competed in Helsinki.

1958: The opening meet at the Clonliffe Harriers' Santry Stadium, the first purpose built athletics stadium in Ireland, was held on 19–20 May 1958. The inspiration of Billy Morton who staged a series of high-profile international athletics meetings at College Park and Lansdowne Road to fund the development, the new venue's running track was a replica of the Olympic track at Melbourne and was installed by the En-Tous-Cas firm from Leicester. The venue also included two grandstands. The opening sod was turned in June 1957 by the Lord Mayor of Dublin, Robert Briscoe and Olympic champion Ronnie Delany.

1978: On 26 March 1978, John Treacy created a major upset by winning the World Cross-Country Championship title in atrocious conditions at Bellahouston Park, Glasgow with a brilliant run that saw him outpace Alexander Antipov (USSR) by 3 seconds and Karel Lismont (Belgium). A year later, on 25 March 1979, in a highly pressurised situation, before an attendance of 25,000, he successfully defended the title at Green Park Racecourse, Limerick, finishing 7 seconds ahead of Bronislaw Malinowski (Poland) with Antipov in third place. Treacy drew clear of the field at the end of the first lap and 'could not believe how easy it was for me. The whole race was easy from that point onwards. I just floated away from them.' Treacy and Tim Smythe are the only male Irish athletes to have won world cross-country titles.

1980: The Dublin Marathon, organised by the Business Houses Athletic Association (BHAA), was held for the first time. The BHAA, a voluntary organisation set up by running groups from businesses, allowed athletes from both BLE and NACAI to compete together under the one banner. The visionary Noel Carroll persuaded Alex Sweeney, the chairman of the BHAA, to undertake the organisation of the event. The first race attracted an entry of 2,001 competitors including sixty women was won by Dick Hooper with Carey May, the first woman home. Jim Aughney succeeded Alex Sweeney as race director in 1997. From 1998, the marathon has successfully attracted international runners: in 2000 more runners from the USA than from Ireland competed. In 2002, the race series was introduced to help runners prepare for the marathon over a series of shorter races. In the 25th anniversary race of 2004 entries reached 10,000. The Dublin Marathon was held for the first time on a Sunday in 2016 and 19,500 runners entered, over 16,800 finished making the event the fourth largest in Europe behind London, Berlin and Paris. The winners include Ireland's Olympic medallists John Treacy (1993) and Sonia O'Sullivan (2000).

1984: 3 July 1984. A magic night in the Mardyke that outshone Santry Stadium's hot August night of 1958 for its athletic magnificence. Russian athletes Yuriy Sedykh and Sergey Litvinov were the outstanding figures of hammer throwing in the 1980s and the two came together at the Quinnsworth Cork City Sports on 3 July. Litvinov was the world record holder (84.14m) and world champion (1983), Sedykh, the Olympic (1976, 1980) and European champion, when the head-to-head took place in the mother country of hammer throwing. Sedykh ended the contest early and smashed the world record with a massive opening throw of 86.34m. The existing world record was surpassed five more times on the night. Litvinov threw 85.20m and 84.84m with his second and third efforts; Syedikh followed his initial effort with record smashing throws of 86.00m, 85.20m and 84.16m before throwing 83.30m with his last valid throw.

Three new Irish national records were also established on the night, the most noteworthy by Caroline O'Shea. Running in only her fourth 800m race, O'Shea produced a truly great performance to finish in third place behind two Russian athletes and achieved the Olympic qualifying time with the new national record of 2:00.70, a time that has only been twice bettered, by Sonia O'Sullivan and Rose-Anne Galligan, since then.

1990: Ireland's first indoor athletics arena was opened on 23 December. Sean Naughton spearheaded the development of the Nenagh Olympic Club's facility of eight lanes for sprints and hurdles and a 200m track banked at the bends. Appropriately Eamonn Coghlan was given the honour of running the first two laps of the track in what Ronnie Delany described as 'a fantastic day for Irish athletics'.

2011: 21 November 2011 is one of the dark days in Irish athletic history, as the UCD authorities abruptly announced the closure of the Belfield athletic track 'due to health and safety concerns', citing a badly worn surface that became 'slippy when wet'. Hours later, JCBs excavated trenches in the track ensuring it was no longer fit for purpose. In June 2011, a section was converted to a pay-per-use car park. When opened on 14 June 1977, the Belfield track was the first tartan track in the Republic of Ireland.

2014: Apart from those previously documented, three Irish athletes Roisín McGettigan (European Indoor Championships 2009, 1,500m), Rob Heffernan (European Championships 2010, 20km walk) and Derval O'Rourke (European Indoor Championships 2013, 60m hurdles) had their positions upgraded to bronze-medal status because of the doping infractions of the original podium occupiers.

BIBLIOGRAPHY

BOOKS

Barry, John Joe, *The Ballincurry Hare* (Athletic Publications, 1981).

Bracken, Patrick, *The Growth and Development of Sport, 1840–1880*, Unpublished PhD Thesis, De Montfort University, Leicester, 2014.

Branigan, Dominic, *Clonliffe Harriers, Athletics Club 1886–2013* (Original Writing, 2013).

Buchanan, Ian, *The A.A.A. Championships 1880–1939* (National Union of Track Statisticians, 2003).

Coghlan, Eamonn, with George Kimball, *Eamonn Coghlan: Chairman of the Boards, Master of the Mile* (Red Rock Press, 2008).

Corry, Eoghan, *Kildare GAA: A Centenary History* (Kildare GAA Board, 1984).

de Búrca, Marcus, *The G.A.A: A History of the Gaelic Athletics Association* (Gill Books, 1980).

Delany, Ronnie, *Staying the Distance* (The O'Brien Press, 2006).

Fleming, Liam, *Cork Champions Past and Present* (Self-Published, 2013).

Griffin, Padraig, *The Politics of Irish Athletics, 1850–1990* (Marathon Publications, 1990).

Guiney, David, *Gold, Silver and Bronze* (PR Books, n.d.).

Hauman, Riël, 'Kennedy Kane McArthur: Invincible Marathoner' in *South African Athletics Annual*, 2012.

Henry, Noel, *From Sophie to Sonia: A History of Irish Women's Athletics* (Noel Henry, 1998).

Heffernan, Robert, *Walking Tall: The Autobiography of a World Champion and Olympic Medallist* (Collins Press, 2016).

Hornbuckle, Adam R., 'Matthew McGrath' in John A. Garraty and Mark C. Carnes (eds), *American National Biography*, vol. 15 (Oxford University Press, 1999).

Hymans, Richard and Imre Matrahazi, *Progression of IAAF World Records – 2015 Edition* (IAAF, 2015).

Katchen, Alan S., *Abel Kiviat, National Champion; Twentieth-Century Track and Field and the Melting Pot* (Syracuse University Press, 2009).

Lawson, Gerald, *World Record Breakers in Track & Field Athletics* (Human Kinetics, 1997).

Lovesey, Peter, *The Official Centenary History of the Amateur Athletics Association* (Guinness Superlatives, 1980).

Lucas, Charles J.P., *The Olympic Games 1904, St Louis Mo. USA* (Woodward & Tiernan, 1905).

McCarthy, Kevin, *Gold, Silver and Green: the Irish Olympic Journey 1896–1924* (Cork University Press, 2010).

McKiernan, Catherina, with Ian O'Riordan, *Catherina McKiernan: Running for my Life* (Red Rock Press, 2005).

Murphy, Colm, *The Irish Championships, 1873–1884: The ICAC and the DAC Championships* (Self-published, 2004).

Naughton, Lindie, *Lady Icarus: The Life of Irish Aviator Lady Mary Heath* (Ashfield Press, 2004).

Naughton, Lindie, 'Irish Women's Athletics and the Olympic Games' in *History Ireland*, vol. 20, no. 4, July–August 2012.

O'Donoghue, Tony, *Irish Championship Athletics, 1873–1914* (Self-published, n.d.).

Ó Riain, Séamus, *Maurice Davin (1842–1927): First President of the GAA* (Geography Publications, n.d.).

O'Riordan, Ian, *Miles to Run, Promises to Keep* (Boglark Press, 2010).

O'Sullivan, Sonia, with Tom Humphries, *Sonia: My Story* (Penguin, Ireland, 2008).

Peters, Mary, with Ian Wooldridge, *Mary P. Autobiography* (Arrow Books Ltd, 1976 ed.).

Quercetani, Roberto L., *Athletics: A History of Modern Track and Field Athletics: 1860–1990* (Vallardi and Asociati, 1990).

Quinn, Mark, *The King of Spring* (The Liffey Press, 2004).

Redmond, Patrick R., *The Irish and the Making of American Sport* (McFarland & Co., 2014).

Rouse, Paul, *Sport and Ireland: A History* (Oxford University Press, 2015).

Siggins, Gerard, and Malachy Clerkin, *Lansdowne Road* (The O'Brien Press, 2010).

Tisdall, R.M.N., and Fenn Sherie, *The Young Athlete* (Blackie, 1934).

Wallechinsky, David, and Jamie Loucky, *The Complete Book of the Olympics* (Aurum Press, 2012).

Zarnowski, Frank, 'Thomas F. Kiely – A Biography' *in Journal of Olympic History*, no. 2, vol. 14 (2006).

NEWSPAPERS, MAGAZINES AND PERIODICALS

Cork Examiner
Freemans Journal
History Ireland
Holly Bough
Irish Examiner
Irish Independent
Irish Press
Irish Runner
Irish Times
Marathon Magazine
Munster Express
Nenagh Guardian
New York Times
Sports Illustrated
Track and Field News
Tuam Herald

WEBSITES

www.annadalestriders.co.uk/Interviews
www.athleticsireland.ie
www.bringbackthemile.com
www.marathonmac2012.com/kk-mcarthur-story.aspx
www.runningpast.com/wanamaker_mile.htm
www.secsports.com/article/11169032/mcgovern-born-run
www.usatf.org
www.ustfccca.org/assets/record-book/ncaa-division-i-indoor-track/
    NCAA-DI-ITF-Event-YearByYearResults.pdf
www.trackandfieldnews.com
www.villanovarunning.blogspot.ie